Model-Driven Testing

Paul Baker · Zhen Ru Dai · Jens Grabowski ·
Øystein Haugen · Ina Schieferdecker ·
Clay Williams

Model-Driven Testing

Using the UML Testing Profile

With 94 Figures and 4 Tables

 Springer

Authors

Paul Baker
Motorola Labs
Jays Close
Viables Industrial Estate
Basingstoke
Hampshire, RG22 4PD, UK
Paul.Baker@motorola.com

Zhen Ru Dai
Ina Schieferdecker
Fraunhofer Fokus
Kaiserin-Augusta-Allee 31
10589 Berlin, Germany
dai@fokus.fraunhofer.de
schieferdecker@fokus.fraunhofer.de

Jens Grabowski
Institute for Computer Science
University of Goettingen
Lotzestrasse 16-18
37083 Göttingen, Germany
grabowski@cs.uni-goettingen.de

Øystein Haugen
Department of Informatics
University of Oslo
P.O. Box 1080, Blindern
0316 Oslo, Norway
oysteinh@ifi.uio.no

Clay Williams
19 Skyline Drive
Hawthorne, NY 10532
USA
clayw@us.ibm.com

ACM Computing Classification: D.2, K.6

ISBN 978-3-642-09159-9   e-ISBN 978-3-540-72563-3

Springer is a part of Springer Science+Business Media
springer.com
© Springer-Verlag Berlin Heidelberg 2010

Cover Design: KünkelLopka, Heidelberg

Foreword

Psychologists have a phrase for the human ability to believe two completely contradictory things at the same time; it is called "cognitive dissonance." We do seem to be quite capable of believing that war is evil (though we should destroy our enemies), taxes are too high (though government spending should increase), and that politicians can keep a promise (perhaps enough said on that point). Psychologists in fact tell us that this ability to simultaneously face and ignore realities makes it possible to live in a complicated, constantly changing world. Engineers, however, are supposed to do better than live in hope. Engineers model systems, test their models against requirements, execute their designs, and then test their models against the post-development reality (e.g., system design versus as-built) to ensure the quality and sustainability of their product and in fact their production methods. Why, then, do we in the computer engineering field find ourselves with an enormous software quality problem, all over the world?

I've just finished reading an article in a leading software development magazine about the state of the software testing industry, which leads off with the unlikely sentence, "The ethos of quality is sweeping into the IT space..."[1]. I had to read the line several times before I realized that it did not read, "the ethos of quality has swept completely out to space," which I think is the more likely position! Software quality–measured either qualitatively or quantitatively–is atrocious, in nearly all settings, whether commercial, academic, or open-source. The level of concern for customer needs, even customer *safety,* is surprisingly small. Major software vendors beta-test (and even alpha-test) their software by placing it in the hands of millions of customers, many of whom are paying for the software they are testing. "Don't buy version 1.0," is the common credo of most Chief Information Officers that I know.

---

[1] "The Trouble with Software QC: Steps toward making better software better," by Colin Armitage, in Dr Dobb's Journal, March 2007.

Where might the solution to this problem lie? Certainly, there are several different foci needed to solve the problem, and the most important is a changing point of view (and therefore incentivization and management style) on the part of customers and development labs, a point of view that software quality is important and in fact might be worth paying for. These market issues, coupled with developer commitment to software quality expressed in process and methodology, will make a difference.

But technology plays a part also. In particular, the move to Model-Driven Architecture (MDA) as a basis for engineering software-based systems shows some promise to help support corporate commitments to quality. Although MDA originally focused primarily on software delivery, maintenance, and integration, with the intent of lowering the costs involved in those phases of the software lifecycle (especially maintenance and integration), the MDA approach has something to say about software testing as well.

Think back, for a moment, to what engineers did (and still do) when engineering meant purely nuts, bolts, steel, wood, and concrete. An architect or structural engineer would specify materials for, for example, bridge construction, including such things as steel tensile strength and admixture minima in the concrete mix. While these specifications—abstractions, or models— are used in various artifacts of the construction process (e.g., requests for quotation, requests for proposals, bills of materials, bills of lading), they are also used by responsible engineers in the test phase of construction. When the concrete appears on the job site, samples are tested to ensure that the admixture delivered meets the requirements specified in the construction plans. If it does not, a potential disaster awaits, as the entire structure may very well depend on the concrete block about to be poured. This lesson was learned in unfortunate detail throughout the 19th century, as the failings of cast iron as a bridge-building material (due to fracture) was slowly understood.

The key idea here, however, is not about bridge-building but about *tests based on designs*. Clearly, we should be doing the same thing in the software field if we are to be considered "engineers" in the same class as civil engineers and chemical engineers!

This concept of model-driven testing, of extending the concepts of tests based on designs (borrowed from older engineering fields) to *software* designs, has been a major focus area recently at OMG and is carefully expanded upon in the book you are holding. Once one has a system design—for a road bridge or for a bridge-playing program!—one should be able to specify in those requirements how to test the as-built artifact (the running code) to ensure that it meets the requirements of the intended (and often unintended) users.

Software modeling is not a trivial subject, and extending modeling to the automatic generation not only of code but of software unit and integration tests is not any simpler. This book, however, does an admirable job of integrating the concepts of modeling and testing and leverages the latest standards and technologies to help you make your software testing regime and process better, faster, and cheaper. It is worth the read.

The problem with politicians, however, remains for a better day!

Richard Mark Soley, PhD
Chairman and CEO
Object Management Group, Inc.
April 25, 2007

Preface

As software systems become more important in almost every facet of human life, the demand for software quality increases. As a result, several new technologies have emerged to help with the development of high-quality, systems. These include UML for system specification, JUnit, and TTCN-3 for test case design and execution, as well as new development paradigms such as Model-Driven Architecture (MDA).

Prior to the development of the UML Testing Profile (UTP), there was not a test specification language that aligned UML and other technologies such as those mentioned above. The consortium of institutions involved in the development of the UTP (Ericsson, Fraunhofer/FOKUS, IBM/Rational, Motorola, Telelogic, University of Lübeck) sought to address this absence by providing a UML profile for test specification. This book represents the first comprehensive introduction to the standard.

We would like to thank Telelogic AB for providing us with the Telelogic TAU tool for use in creating the diagrams in this book. We also want to thank Eric Samuelsson, our colleague at Telelogic, who was invaluable in developing the profile. He was unable to participate in the writing of this book, but his wise guidance during the development of the profile informs much of the material in this work. Finally, we want to thank our editor at Springer, Ralf Gerstner, for giving us a chance to publish the work and for providing us with careful guidance during the process.

Paul Baker	Winchester, UK,
Zhen Ru Dai	Berlin, Germany,
Jens Grabowski	Göttingen, Germany,
Øystein Haugen	Oslo, Norway,
Ina Schieferdecker	Berlin, Germany,
Clay Williams	New York, NY,
April 2007	

Contents

Part VI Appendixes

Introduction

As software systems become increasingly complex, new paradigms are needed for their construction. One of these new paradigms is model-driven development, which already has a demonstrable impact in reducing time to market and improving product quality. This particular paradigm is concerned with the introduction of rigorous models throughout the development process, enabling abstraction and automation. To this end a standardized, graphical language called the *Unified Modeling Language* (UML)[TM] was developed by the IT and software industry for the construction of software systems. UML enables system requirement and design specifications to be created and visualized in a graphical manner, which supports improved communication and validation. It also enables the introduction of automated software production techniques. As a consequence, UML has become widely adopted as a development technology throughout the software industry.

However, the development of high-quality systems requires not only systematic development processes but also systematic test processes. This book is specifically about systematic, model-based test processes in the context of UML. As UML provides only limited means for the design and development of corresponding tests, a consortium was built by the *Object Management Group* (OMG) in order to develop a *Unified Modeling Language, version 2* (UML 2) profile to enable model-based testing with UML [24, 36]. We refer to this profile as the *UML Testing Profile* (UTP).

With the resulting UTP, the way models and their realizations can be tested and evaluated has been unified. Dedicated test concepts help to design and structure tests, to define test procedures and related test data precisely. The profile also allows users to derive and reason about the quality of tests and about the test coverage of a given test suite. The UTP closes a gap in the set of technologies around UML: It combines and integrates system and test development via UML and provides a common way for the different stakeholders to communicate and reason about the systems and their tests with which they are involved as developers, purchasers, customers, and users. The profile also allows system architects, designers, and developers to efficiently cooperate with the testers throughout the system development process on the basis of a common model base.

Six organizations consisting of tool vendors, industrial users, and research institutes (Ericsson, Fraunhofer FOKUS, IBM/Rational, Motorola, Telelogic and University of Goettingen to Lubeck) decided to collaborate and produce the UTP specification jointly. While some of the consortium members come from the world of testing, others are experienced in system modeling with *Message Sequence Chart* (MSC), *Specification and Description Language* (SDL), and UML, respectively. These members agreed that by working in a larger team, the resultant profile would have a broader scope on testing, where the best ideas should be incorporated into the profile specification. After 2 years' work, the UTP specification has been adopted by the OMG [35]. Since summer 2005, the profile has become an official standard at the OMG [26].

In this book, we present how UML is used for the purposes of testing complex software systems. We introduce a systematic but simple methodology for addressing different types of testing within UML-based development. The book helps avoiding typical difficulties in designing, structuring, and developing tests systematically: UTP is introduced stepwise–driven by a case study that highlights the principles and concepts of the underlying methodology. The important issues of test completeness, correctness, and consistency are discussed. The book teaches the reader how to use the UTP for test modeling and test specification. It presents best practices for using UML for different aspects of testing and demonstrates the automated execution of UML-based tests with existing test frameworks such as the JUnit test framework for Java and *Testing and Test Control Notation* (TTCN-3).

To aid the reader, we introduce three types of highlighted text within the book:

1. **UTP Concepts.** These are presented to the reader as we introduce concepts from the UTP standard.
2. **UTP Methodology.** These denote key process aspects the reader should consider when using UTP.
3. **UTP Tips.** These are include to highlight pertinant or key points that are very useful or important when using or considering UTP.

Everyone involved in software quality assurance could benefit from the techniques introduced in this book. The book helps testers understand the concepts of UTP and applying it within a UML-based system development process. The book is

- for *testers and developers* who are looking to use model-based and automated testing or that are in organizations using UML for software system development;
- for *project managers, system architects, and designers* who want to address system quality and testability aspects throughout system development;

- for *students and academics* wishing to learn about testing with UML; and
- for *tool developers* wishing to get an overview of how tools can support UML-based testing.

Although UML is briefly introduced at the beginning of the book, it is advantageous for readers to be familiar with UML—for example, as described in [29].

We recommend reading this book sequentially from start to end. UML experts and those being less interested in the specific details of the case study may decide to start with Part II on *functional testing*. If you are interested in *advanced testing concepts*, for example, how to design test data efficiently or how to do performance, load, and scalability testing, you might start reading with Part III. *General aspects of applying UTP* are discussed in Part IV. Tools are covered in Part V and Section 11.1, respectively. Part VI provides an overview of a UTP reference guide, a list of acronyms, an index, and references.

Part I

Foundations

1

Model-Based Testing

Wikipedia [41], the free encyclopedia on the World Wide Web (www), refers to model-based testing as *"software testing where test cases are derived in whole or in part from a model that describes some (if not all) aspects of the system under test (SUT)"* [39]. The SUT may be something as simple as a method or class, or as complex as a complete system or a solution consisting of multiple systems. For testing, a model provides a behavioral description of the SUT.[1] This description can be processed to yield a set of test cases that can be used to determine whether the SUT conforms to a desirable property that is represented in the model. In this chapter, we identify the phases in the software development process where models are designed and describe the principles of test development based on models.

1.1 The Software Development Process

Literature distinguishes between different software development processes. Examples of such processes are the software life cycle, the waterfall model, the spiral model, the unified process, the V-model, and the W-model [33, 34, 40]. In all these different processes, software is developed in phases. Most of the processes have similar phases and mainly differ in the conditions and possibilities for progressing into the next phase or revisiting a previous phase. A specialty of the V- and W-models is an integrated view of construction and corresponding testing phases. In this book, we use V- and W-models to explain model-based testing and the role of UML Testing Profile (UTP) in the software development process.

---

[1] A model is an abstraction of a complex problem or system which should be solved or implemented in software or hardware. Behavioral descriptions are only one aspect of a model; further aspects may be related to structural and non-functional requirements.

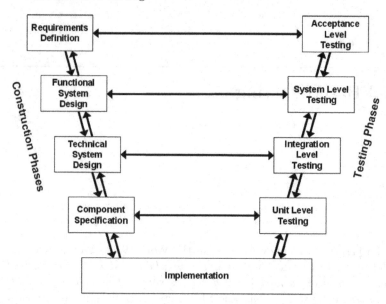

Fig. 1.1. The V-model

The principle structure of the V-model is shown in Figure 1.1. The V-model distinguishes between construction phases (shown on the left-hand side in Figure 1.1) and testing phases (right-hand side in Figure 1.1).

System development starts with the *Requirements Definition* phase. Requirements are captured from the customer and future users. They are used in the following *Functional System Design* phase to develop a functional model of the system. The functional model should be independent from the future implementation of the system to avoid early design decisions. It may include artifacts from the environment of the system and even business processes of the customer. The software architecture is modeled in the *Technical System Design* phase. This phase structures the software system into components and defines the interfaces among the constituents. The detailed behavior of the components is defined in the *Component Specification* phase. The construction phases of the V-model end with the *Implementation* of the components.

The implementation of the components is the basis for the following testing phases. In the *Unit Level Testing* phase, component implementations are tested against their specifications. In the next step, *Integration Level Testing* is used to test the smooth interworking of the finalized components. The integration testing phase ends when all components are integrated and the complete system is ready for *System Level Testing*. System level testing is the first test where the complete system is available and the complete functionality is tested. The basis for system level testing is the functional system design but may also include tests from the perspective of the developers and system integrators. *Acceptance Level Testing* is very similar to system level testing but is purely based on the perspective of the customer and the future users.

Even though the V-model suggests a procedure where the testing phases are performed after the construction phases, it is well known that the preparation of each testing phase should start as early as possible, that is, in parallel to the corresponding construction phase. This allows for early feedback regarding the testing phase. The W-model [33], illustrated in Figure 1.2, is a refinement of the V-model.

On the left-hand side of the W-model, the construction phases are structured into two tasks: (1) a construction task and (2) a corresponding test preparation task. The arrows between construction and test preparation tasks indicate iterations during the work on these tasks.

The right-hand side of the W-model covers test execution and debugging. The arrows between test execution, debugging, and implementation describe the iterative correction of errors. If a test detects a failure, debugging is needed to locate the fault and after correcting the fault, that is, changing the implementation, the test has to be executed again.

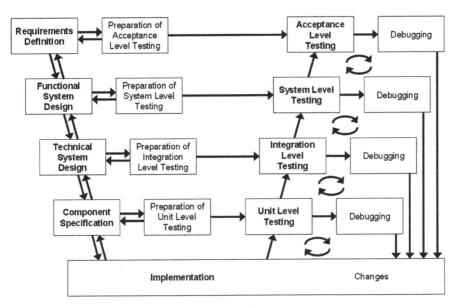

Fig. 1.2. The W-model

1.2 UML and UTP in System Development

The results of the work on the different phases in the software development process are artifacts describing a software system at different levels of abstraction and from different perspectives. The artifacts are *models* of the system.

The models may be defined by using different languages and notations. For example, the requirements may be defined by using plain English text, a programming language such as C++ may be used for the implementation, and a script language may implement executable test cases.

This book is about models and modeling languages. We follow the approach that only one modeling language is used, the UML. The exhaustive usage of UML allows the usage of commercial UML tools and eases communication between the customer and the people working in a project team. Commercial UML tools provide several potential advantages. They may support domain-specific UML profiles, they allow consistency checks between UML models produced in different construction phases, and they often have facilities to generate test cases and implementations. We are aware of the fact that not all artifacts should be written in the form of UML diagrams (e.g., user guidelines) and that not all requirements can be expressed adequately with UML (e.g., robustness or usability criteria). However, UML tools are evolving, and experience has shown that the use of UML improves the quality of the software products and the software development process.

While we cover the basics of UML, this book is about UTP. UTP is a specialization of UML for testing. It provides testing concepts in UML and therefore eases the communication between developers and testers. Our UML-centric view of the W-model is shown in Figure 1.3. *Pure* UML should be used in the constructions tasks, and UTP should be applied in the test preparation tasks of the W-model. In this book, we explain the concepts of UTP and explain how UTP models can be derived systematically from UML models.

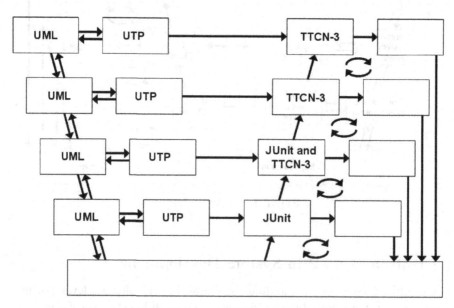

Fig. 1.3. Using UML and UTP in system development

Figure 1.3 also refers to the Testing and Test Control Notation (TTCN-3) and JUnit, because UTP provides mapping rules to both testing technologies. JUnit, a testing framework for Java implementations, is mainly used for tests close to the implementations, that is, for unit level testing and integration level testing. The domain of TTCN-3 is functional black-box testing of communication systems. Therefore, TTCN-3 is often applied in later testing phases, that is, for integration testing of subsystems, system level testing, and acceptance level testing. The mapping of UTP to JUnit and TTCN-3 will be explained in Chapters 12 and 13 of this book.

1.3 Model-Based Test Development

Model-based testing requires the systematic and possibly automatic derivation of tests from models. In our case, UML is the language for specifying models and UTP the formalism to describe the derived tests.

From a testing perspective, UML models can be seen as software programs. Therefore, the test derivation approaches known from general software testing can also be applied to UML models. The two basic techniques in software testing are *black-box testing* and *white-box testing*. The principles of black-box and white-box testing are well described in, for example, the books of Beizer [1] and Myers [20].

In addition to these techniques, several methods for the automatically generating test cases from formal description techniques exist. These methods may be applicable to UML models if the models are executable and if a formal semantics for the used subset of UML exists. The automatic generation of tests from UML models cannot be covered in this book, because it is still an actual research topic [7].

1.3.1 Black-Box Testing Approaches

Black-box testing, often also called *functional testing*, treats the SUT as a black box. Tests are developed without any assumption about the internal structure of the SUT. They evaluate the pure input–output behavior of the SUT. Typically, a set of test cases is defined for each function of the SUT, focusing on the different outputs which the function should produce.

Well-known approaches for the systematic development of black-box tests are *equivalence class partitioning* and *boundary value analysis*. For equivalence class partitioning, the domain of each input parameter of a function is structured into equivalence classes. For the values in an equivalence class, it is assumed that the function treats them in the same manner, and therefore, only one representative of each equivalence class needs to be tested. Boundary value analysis is often used in combination with equivalence class partitioning. In this approach, test cases developed by equivalence class partitioning are supplemented by test cases that test the boundaries of the equivalence classes because typical programming errors, for example, wrong termination conditions for loops, are often related to these boundaries.

In UML, functions are specified on different levels of abstraction. Use cases describe the main functionality of the entire system, that is, on system level, and methods of classes specify functions on subsystem and unit level. The different levels of abstraction correspond to the different construction and testing phases described in the V-model — see Figure 1.1. In other words, use cases and methods identify the sets of test cases which have to be developed for achieving a functional coverage of the system. Help for the identification of equivalence classes may be given by the detailed specification of use cases and methods by, for example, sequence diagrams or activity diagrams. The specified flows of control are often related to equivalence classes.

1.3.2 White-Box Testing Approaches

White-box testing (also called *glass-box testing*) makes use of the internal structure of the SUT, that is, treats the SUT as glass box. Test cases are developed by using coverage criteria for the program code. Typical coverage criteria are statement coverage, branch coverage, and path coverage. Further coverage criteria are related to the usage of variables in the program flow and conditions that determine branching and loop termination.

Coverage criteria may also be used for deriving test cases from UML models. For example, state and transition coverage criteria can be used to define a satisfactory set of test cases for a state machine describing the behavior of a class. Coverage criteria may also be used to define test cases for sequence diagrams, activity diagrams, and interaction overview diagrams.

1.3.3 Automatic Test Generation

Automatic test generation requires a specification language which has a formal semantics, such as a semantics based on *Finite State Machines* (FSM). The principles of an FSM-based automatic test generation are the following: The semantics of an FSM-based language describes how a specification written in that language can be translated automatically into a corresponding FSM that describes the behavior of the specified system. Automatic test generation assumes that an implementation, which implements such a specification, has the same properties as the FSM, for example, states and state transitions. The algorithms for automatic test generation take advantage of this assumption by simulating the FSM and searching for sequences which are characteristic for states and state transitions of the FSM. A short summary of FSM-based test generation can be found in, for example, the book of Holzmann [12].

FSMs are only one possibility to describe the formal semantics of a specification language. Other languages use labeled transition systems, abstract state machines, or Petri nets. However, the automatic test generation process is very similar for all formalisms. This means a specification is translated into the formal model and the test generation algorithm search for traces which demonstrate certain properties of the model. These traces form the basis for the test behavior.

The definition of a formal and executable semantics for UML is still under investigation. Therefore, there is no universal approach for automatic test generation from UML models. However, specific approaches based on varying semantic models do exist. These are based on approaches such as using characterizing sequences for states and state transitions to guide test development for model elements such as UML state and activity diagrams.

2

Basics

To read this book, it does help to have some background in both testing and modeling with UML, but we do not require the reader to be fluent in any of these disciplines. Here we provide a brief introduction to the UML modeling language. We also provide the reader with an overview of the UML Testing Profile (UTP), its motivation, and history. Readers with prior knowledge may either read this chapter quickly or skip it altogether.

2.1 UML Overview

This section gives a basic introduction to UML. This is not a complete UML textbook but a brief introduction to the parts of the language applied in this book. For a more detailed description of UML 2, we refer to textbooks that are made specific for that purpose. For a fairly precise description of the language, we recommend [29]. For a quick but fairly accurate glance of what UML 2 is, we suggest [42], and for a full definition of the language, refer to the standard [36].

2.1.1 Introduction to Class Models

If you only know a little UML, you will probably know about class models. Class models are used to define concepts and their associations, and thereby describe the conceptual foundation for a system. Often class models are the diagrams used in the very early phases of development. They are applied in the early stages and form the basis on which the total model is built. Here are the major constructs related to class diagrams.

In Figure 2.1, a number of class symbols are illustrated, named *Y*, *A*, *D*, *E*, *B*, *Super*, and *C*. We also show signals *m1*, *m2*, *m3*, *m4*, and *m5*. Signals are special classes to describe the objects transmitted in asynchronous messaging. Notice that signals look like plain classes, but they are marked with a text

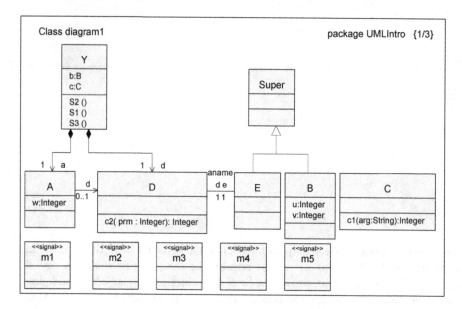

Fig. 2.1. Class diagram—with some signals

«signal» before the name. Such explanatory marks in guillemets are called **stereotypes** and give additional information for the language analyzer. A class symbol contains a number of horizontal compartments, each of which contains a specific kind of information. Observe class Y and notice the entities b:B and c:C. These represent properties that may be interpreted as attributes or internal variables to all Y objects. b has the type B and c has the type C.

Observe class D and notice the entity $c2()$ indicating an **operation** named $c2$. An operation is a specification of a piece of behavior. It is the signature of a unit of behavior and associated with the definition of that behavior. We shall return to the description of behavior later. We find an operation also in class C where the operation $c1$ has a string parameter and returns an Integer result.

However, the lines between the class symbols are as important as the class symbols themselves. Observe the line between classes D and E. This is an **association** decorated with the name $aname$, role names are labeled d and e, and multiplicities are defined as 1. The association name is just there to make it simple to talk about that association. The role names are attached to the association ends. Intuitively, the role name e indicates how D refers to E along the association $aname$. The multiplicities on the association indicate how many objects of one class at a given end of the association may be connected to one object at the other end. In this case, a 1-1 multiplicity association indicates that for each D there is an $aname$ link to one E and vice versa.

Observe the directed line between classes A and D. The direction of the line shows what is called *navigability*, indicating that in the actual object model there must be a straightforward way to come from an A object to a D object. In simple systems, this is implemented as a pointer. The 0..1 multiplicity says that for each A object there may be either 0 or 1 D objects.

Observe the line between classes Y and E. That line has a black diamond at Y and an arrow at E. The arrow again indicates navigability, while the black diamond defines *composition*. A composition means that there are E objects comprised in Y objects and that the lifespan of these E objects cannot extend beyond the lifespan of the Y object containing them. Instead of a black diamond we can use a white diamond to define *aggregation* meaning containment where the contained objects may have a lifespan that extends beyond that of the container.

Finally, observe the relationships between classes E, B, and *Super*. This part of the figure shows two independent constructs.

1. It illustrates that the lines may merge. In the diagram, the lines from E and B merge before they reach the open arrowhead on *Super*. This is graphical shorthand for reducing graphical complexity of the diagram. Semantically, this is equivalent to two lines both ending with an open arrowhead at Super.
2. The open arrowhead defines *generalization*, meaning that classes E and B are *specializations* of *Super*. They inherit all properties of the general class *Super*. This construct is used to define inheritance hierarchies.

One class diagram does not necessarily tell the whole story about the classes shown in it. Rather, the definition of a class is the union of all diagrams involving that class.

In Figure 2.2, we see that class Y has been repeated. It is now involved with class X through an anonymous association and class World through a composition. Both of these relationships add to the definition of class Y. Thus, all new information in any diagram adds to the definition of a concept, and in fact additional information may be added directly into the UML repository model without going through any diagram. A UML tool normally provides a model explorer where the different constructs are presented and where additional language objects may be added and modified.

In Figure 2.3, an *internal structure*, also known as a *composite structure*, for the *World* class is defined. This structure contains two parts x and y of types X and Y. The two parts are also properties of *World* and appear also as the role names of the two composition associations from *World*. Between the parts x and y, there are two connectors that indicate communication between x and y in both directions. The composite structure with x and y could also have been presented within a special compartment of class *World*. The composite structure of class Y is shown in Figure 2.4.

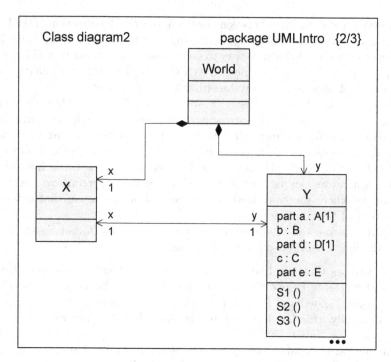

Fig. 2.2. Class diagram—the World

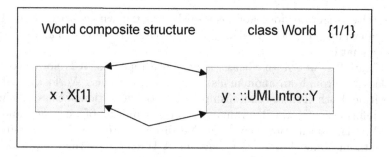

Fig. 2.3. W's composite structure diagram

2.1.2 Introduction to Use Cases

One of the original contributions to UML was **use cases**. Use cases are mostly applied in the initial analysis phases to define what services (or "use cases") the system will provide.

We have given a simple example in Figure 2.5 that says that an actor of type X is involved in a use case describing some functionality $S4$ of the subject $y:Y$. In Section 2.1.3, we define this functionality using other UML notations.

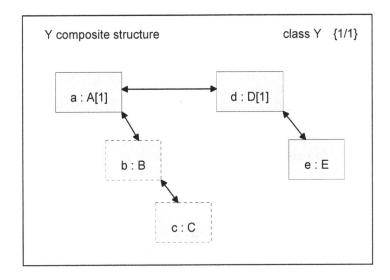

Fig. 2.4. Y's composite structure diagram

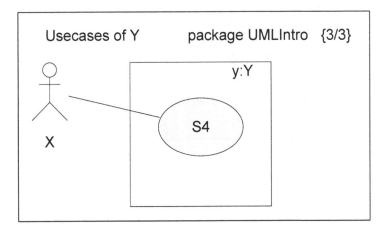

Fig. 2.5. Use cases of Y

Continuing with the use case diagram, the modeler will give the description of the functionality in structured prose. In doing so, *S4* could look like Table 2.1.

The descriptions of use cases are subsequently used by the designers to define the behaviors in more precise UML terms. The use case *S4* is in our case described by a sequence diagram illustrated in Figure 2.9.

Table 2.1. Use case S4

Actors	X
Preconditions	Y must be ready
Normal cases	X will send Y an m1 signal and then Y will return an m4 signal.
Exceptional cases	None

2.1.3 Introduction to Sequence Diagrams

Sequence diagrams, referred to as *interaction diagrams*, have always been in UML. However, the history of interaction diagrams goes back much further than UML. By the 1980s, similar notations were in common use in the large telecom businesses, including Siemens, Ericsson, and Alcatel. The International Telecom Union (*International Telecommunication Union* (ITU)) undertook the task of standardizing such diagrams in the standard Z.120 Message Sequence Charts (MSCs). However, when UML was made, it was based on a slightly different dialect of MSCs. In recent versions of UML, interactions and MSCs are very similar.

In Figure 2.6, we have a frame with a tab in the upper left corner containing the name of the sequence diagram. This frame serves to contain the name and as boundary for messages going in or out of the scenario as a whole. The vertical lines are lifelines, which have names that refer to the parts (or properties) of the class (or collaboration) that owns the behavior described by the sequence diagram. The communication depicted in the diagram must

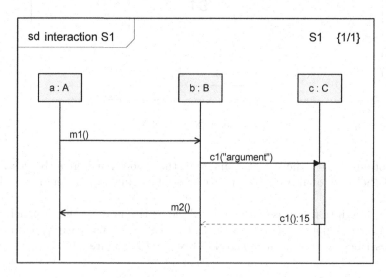

Fig. 2.6. Simplest sequence diagram—S1

be consistent with the connectors of the composite structure of the enclosing classifier (class or collaboration).

The meaning of sequence diagram *S1* is that an object of type *A* sends an asynchronous message to *b* and that *b* in turn calls remotely an operation *c1* in part *c*. The type *C* of *c* will contain an operation *c1* which is triggered with the argument "argument" and which eventually returns with the value 15 in our case. The return of the call takes place after *b* has sent *m2* asynchronously back to *a*. Thus, we distinguish between asynchronous messages depicted by lines with an open arrow head, where the name of the message refers to a signal, and on the other hand remote method invocations depicted by messages with a filled arrow head, where the name of the message refers to an operation of the target lifeline.

Some may wonder how *b* can send message *m2* to object *a* while waiting for the return of remote method invocation *c1*. The reason that this is conceptually possible is that *b* may not consist of only one autonomous object, but may actually comprise several concurrently behaving independent active objects. One of these may perform the call (and wait for the reply), while some other communicates asynchronously with *a*.

Since early versions of UML, sequence diagrams were most often used to describe sequential programs of method invocations; it was commonplace to believe that a sequence diagram described a sequence of messages. This is not usually the general behavior of systems. Even in the very simple example in Figure 2.6, we cannot really determine whether the asynchronous message *m2* is before or after the return message *c1:15*. Furthermore, we must distinguish between the sending of a message and the reception of it. Thus, we must realize that a sequence diagram describes not sequences of messages but rather sequences of events. Events are points on the lifeline, such as the sending of a message or the reception of a message. In Figure 2.6, there are eight different events. The sequencing of events are restricted by two invariants:

1. Events on one lifeline are ordered from the top toward the bottom.
2. The sending of a message must come before the reception of that very message.

As long as these two requirements are met, the ordering of events is arbitrary.

The reason for naming the sequence diagrams is so they can be referenced. In doing so, it is possible to structure complex diagrams into several simpler ones. To reference another sequence diagram, we used something similar to subroutine calls (method calls) or macro expansions of programming languages. In Figure 2.7, we show how *S1* is referred from *S2*. Notice that even though *S1* covered lifelines *b* and *c*, there is no requirement that these lifelines should appear in *S2* as long as there are no message events on them in *S2*. We also notice that message *m1* and *m4* in *S2* come from or go to the environment represented by the frame. This is depicted by having one end of the message on the diagram frame. The environment of a sequence diagram

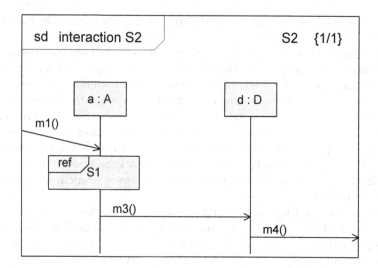

Fig. 2.7. Interaction use—S2

is where it is used. The points on the frame representing interaction points with the environment are called formal gates.

In Figure 2.8, we see that *S2* has been referenced and that the reference has the message *m1* going into it and message *m4* going out of it. These two messages correspond in position and in name with the formal gates of *S2* shown in Figure 2.7. We call the connection points on *S2* actual gates.

After the *S2* reference, there is another frame with the tab name **alt**. This is called a ***combined fragment***. It defines trace alternatives. All traces of *S3* will start with traces from *S2*, because of the reference, and then the traces will go through either the upper operand of the alt-construct or the lower operand. The operands are separated by a dashed operand separator. In Figure 2.8, the two operands end in a ***continuation***. The upper operand ends in *cont1* and the lower operand with *cont2*. Continuations are labels that have significance if *S3* was succeeded by another diagram where operands of the first alt-construct began with continuations *cont1* and *cont2*. Obviously, the meaning is that the traces only follow corresponding continuations.

Combined fragments may have different operators. The other operators are

1. **alt**—alternative traces
2. **opt**—either the traces go through the single operand or it is skipped
3. **par**—parallel merge of the operand traces. Each operand trace remains ordered in the same order, but there may be any permutation between the operands
4. **loop**—loop a number of times (min and max number of iterations may be given)

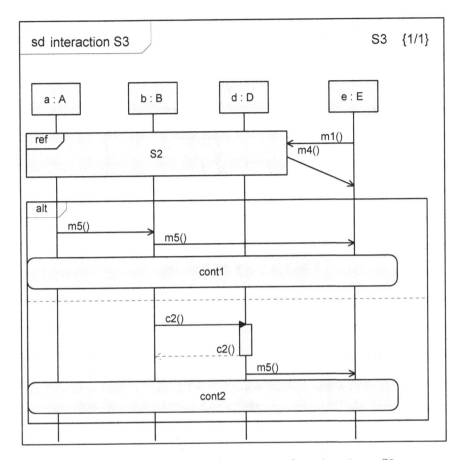

Fig. 2.8. Gates, combined fragments, and continuations—S3

5. **neg**—negative traces, traces that should not happen
6. **assert**—all traces except for those that go through the operand are negative
7. **strict**—ordering of events are exactly as depicted in the diagram regardless of whether the events are on different lifelines or not
8. **ignore**—ignore certain message names
9. **consider**—consider only certain message names
10. **critical**—defines a critical region where events cannot be merged in.

Until now we have introduced a number of structuring mechanisms within sequence diagrams, where we have always focused on the same objects or set of lifelines. But we know that software is often built hierarchically and UML has improved its mechanisms for describing hierarchical architectures. Sequence diagrams can also reap benefits from the architecture hierarchy.

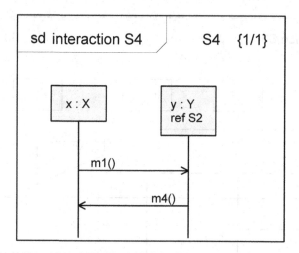

Fig. 2.9. Decomposition—S4

In Figure 2.9, we see a very high-level view. Lifelines x and y communicate via signals $m1$ and $m4$. It is clear that we do not really get much out of such a diagram if we cannot see the insides of at least one of the lifelines. This is where **decomposition** comes into play. Notice the text of lifeline y. It reads "y:Y ref S2," and this means that the details of what goes on within y can be found by looking at sequence diagram *S2*—see Figure 2.7. We see that there is correspondence between the messages going in and out of the lifeline y and the messages going in and out of the sequence diagram S2. In fact, *S2* must be owned by the type Y, and a, b, and c are properties of Y.

Sequence diagrams focus on the interaction between lifelines. The internals of the individual lifelines are often left to other UML diagrams. Still sometimes we feel the need to address attributes of the interacting lifelines. In Figure 2.10, we have augmented *S3* by some data-oriented constructs. Firstly, we have added guards to the operands of the alt-combined-fragment. The guards are predicates that need to evaluate to true for this operand to be valid. The guard must be placed on the lifeline with the first event of the operand. The predicate may refer only to global and constant variables or attributes of the lifeline covered by the guard. In Figure 2.10, the first operand has the guard "[w>7]," which is understandable if w is an attribute of A. The second operand has the guard "[u<17]" and u is an attribute of B. Notice that the operands can have guards on different lifelines within the same combined fragment.

Data values can also occur as parameters to messages. In Figure 2.10, we have shown the operation call c2(u*v) where obviously "u*v" is an input value to the operation. Both u and v are attributes of B (or global variables, e.g., defined within the sequence diagram itself). The return message returns with a value, and the notation given shows what happens with it. "v=c2(-):17" means that the *c2* operation returns the value 17, and this value is assigned to

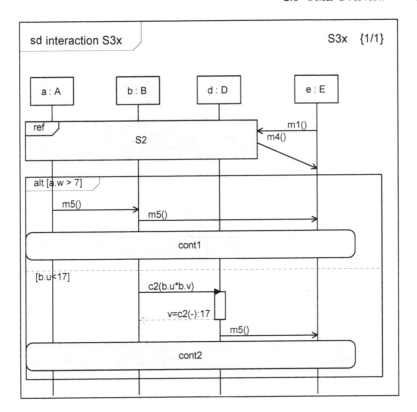

Fig. 2.10. Data: parameters and guards—S3x

attribute *v*. The dash just shows that there is one parameter, but it is an input parameter and not a return parameter. It is commonplace in sequence diagrams to use symbolic names to values since it is usually not the case that one knows exactly what values apply. Here, we could have said "a-prime" instead of "17" to indicate that *c2* would return some (unknown) prime number.

2.1.4 Introduction to State Machines

While sequence diagrams are used to describe the interaction between objects, state machines are used to define the behavior of one object (or a class of objects). State machines are used in many different ways in computer science. The theory of finite state machines has been exploited for many years.

Figure 2.11 shows a very simple state machine that still contains most of the concepts needed. The state machine describes the behavior which is also described by the sequence diagrams by the lifeline a:A. While the sequence diagrams always tell only a partial story, a state machine tells the full story of the behavior of that object. It describes all the behavior that the object can exhibit.

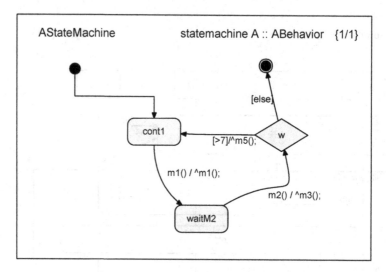

Fig. 2.11. State machine diagram

Let us go through the syntactic elements of Figure 2.11 and thereby explain the behavior of A. In the upper left corner, we find the text AStateMachine which is the name of the behavior. In this case, the behavior is described as a state machine. Still in the upper left part of the frame, we find the initial pseudostate depicted by a filled small circle. This is where the behavior begins once the object has been created. The line from the initial state leads to state symbol with the text Şcont1Ť. The line from the initial state is called the initial transition, and in this case, there is nothing going on during the initial transition. Typically, an initial transition may contain initializations of attributes or initial sending of signals.

States are represented by rectangles with rounded corners. In UML, we have state machines that define a finite set of states and give the states names. In our example, we have two (simple) states "cont1" and "waitM2". The states represent stable situations where the state machine awaits a trigger. Typically, a trigger is a signal reception.

The line between "cont1" and "waitM2" represents a transition which is triggered by the consumption of the signal "m1." The effect of the transition is to send the m1 signal onward. This small piece of behavior can be seen in Figures 2.6 and 2.7 by focusing only on the a:A lifeline. The general syntax for a transition is given by triggers, then slash, then the effect. The effect is described by an activity containing actions such as sending a signal or doing an assignment. UML does not have a full concrete syntax for actions, but we use the convention that sending a signal is shown by a hat symbol before the name of the signal type (followed by arguments).

From the state waitM2, we may follow the transition triggered by m2 (with the effect of sending an m3 signal). This leads to a diamond-shaped decision pseudostate named "w." The decision pseudostate describes the choice between different continuations based on the runtime value of some variables. In our case, there are two alternative continuations guarded either by "[>7]" or by "[else]." The interpretation is clearly that one branch is chosen when "[w>7]" and the other branch in every other case. Notice that the pseudostates do not represent stable situations like (real) states. Pseudostates are nodes in the graph that represent description points dividing transition fragments that together will make up a full transition. The semantics of a state machine says that the state machine should run uninterrupted until it reaches a new stable state. This is what we normally call "run-to-completion" with respect to state machines.

The else-branch from the decision pseudostate leads to yet another circular symbol slightly different from the initial pseudostate. This symbol is a final state. There can be no transitions leading onward from a final state which in the end means that a final state is the end of the behavior of a state machine and it will terminate.

We have in this very brief introduction omitted some mechanisms found in UML 2 state machines. We have not presented hierarchical states where individual states can be decomposed into a full-fledged state machine. Combined with such submachine states, we have entry and exit points representing additional ways to enter and exit from such a complex state supplementing the initial and final states. Furthermore, state may in general have entry and exit activities that are defined to execute when the state is entered (or exited, respectively).

We have also omitted that state machines may have several orthogonal regions. Orthogonal regions come in handy in some scenarios, but their added complexity is such that we have decided not to discuss them here.

2.1.5 Introduction to Activities

Activity diagrams are used to describe behaviors on high or low abstraction levels. Typically, in high-level process modeling, activity diagrams are frequently used, and also in very detailed design of the implementation of operations or the behavior effect of transitions of state machines.

In Figure 2.12, we have shown a very simple activity diagram explaining in some more detail the implementation of the operation c2 in the class D. On the left side of the frame, there are two pin symbols depicting the input parameter and the return value from the operation that together represent the interface of the operation.

Similar to the state machines, we have initial and final nodes representing the start and the finish of the behavior. The symbols with names *double prm* and *add one* are activity symbols where the name actually refers to some underlying activity that is referenced. In our case, the names just represent informal descriptions of what should be done. Since UML does not have any concrete textual syntax for such common tasks as assignments, the names of

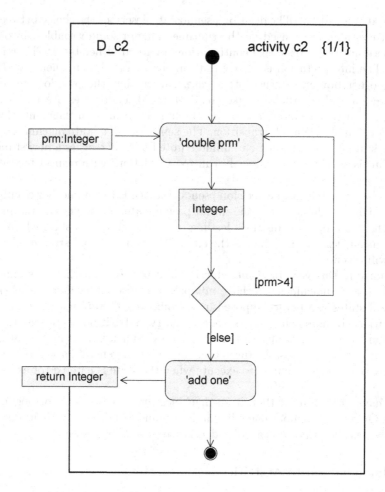

Fig. 2.12. Activity diagram—behavior of operation c2

the activities may be given names as *"prm=prm*2,"* with the obvious intuition originating from Java or C syntax.

The diamond node is again a decision symbol, and the branches have guards, like transitions in state machines. For simple activity diagrams, the interpretation is quite intuitive.

Still activity diagrams have a number of more advanced mechanisms that we have not presented here. You may describe parallel forks, interrupts, and partitions.

2.2 UTP Overview

A UML profile may be seen as a specialization of UML. A profile extends and restricts the original (UML) language. The UTP provides concepts that target the pragmatic development of concise test specifications and test models for testing. In particular, the profile introduces concepts covering test architecture, test behavior, test data, and test time. Together, these concepts define a modeling language for visualizing, specifying, analyzing, constructing, and documenting the artifacts of a test system. The philosophy we adopted for the development of these test concepts has been to make use of existing UML 2.0 concepts wherever possible, thereby minimizing the introduction of new concepts. We identified the supplementary concepts of the testing profile by analyzing existing test specification and test implementation techniques, including JUnit [16] and the Testing and Test Control Notation (TTCN-3) [10].

The test architecture is the definition of all concepts needed to perform the tests. In Figure 2.13, we see that the test architecture package imports the definition of the system under test (SUT), which in our case is contained within the Library system. We also import the testing profile to get access to its predefined concepts such as the Verdict type.

In the test architecture package, we define the test context and the concepts needed to define the tests. In Figure 2.14, we have defined the simulated borrowers and librarians as specializations of the librarian and borrower of the library system context. Furthermore, we have described the test context where the test cases (such as TestBorrowLocallyAvailable) appear as operations.

Figure 2.15 shows the test configuration where test components stimulate the SUT and evaluate the responses. The test configuration is the composite structure of the test context.

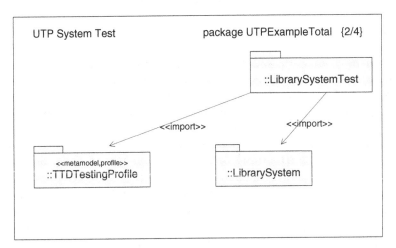

Fig. 2.13. Test architecture

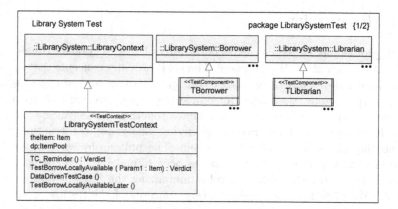

Fig. 2.14. Test package

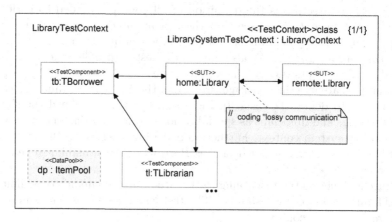

Fig. 2.15. Test configuration

Here is a summary of the concepts briefly presented:

- *Test architecture* is the set of concepts (in addition to the UML 2.0 structural concepts) to specify the structural aspects of a test situation.
- *Test context* is the context of the tests allowing to group test cases, to describe a test configuration, and to define the test control, that is, the required execution order of the test cases.
- *Test configuration* is the composite structure of the test context showing the communication structure between the test components and the system under test.
- *The SUT* where one or more objects within a test specification can be identified as the SUT.
- *Test components*, which are defined as objects within the test system that can communicate with the SUT or other components to realize the test behavior.

In Figure 2.15, we see the test configuration of the test context Library-TestContext. The test configuration contains two test components, tb and tl, a borrower and a librarian. The SUT is comprised of two separate parts, the home and the remote libraries. The parts of the test configuration are marked with stereotypes indicating that they are more than plain UML parts.

Having defined the test structures, the test behaviors specify the actions and evaluations necessary to evaluate the test objective, which describes what should be tested. For example, UML interaction diagrams, state machines, and activity diagrams can be used to define test stimuli, observations from the SUT, test control/invocations, coordination, and actions. When such behaviors are specified, focus is usually given to the definition of normative or expected behaviors. In Figure 2.16, we see two test components stimulating the SUT (the home library). We notice also the timers on the tb lifeline guarding the timing of the responses from the library. Timers are not standard in UML, so this was added in the UTP. The timer concepts supplement the simple time concepts defined by UML 2.0.

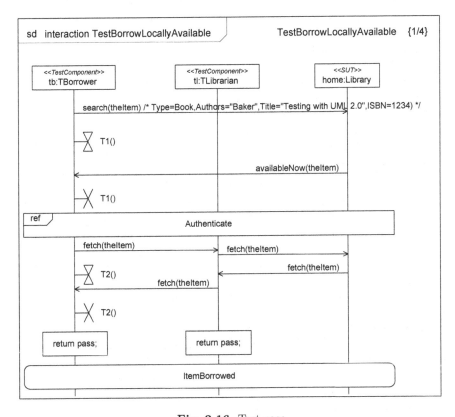

Fig. 2.16. Test case

The UTP introduces concepts for handling unexpected behaviors, providing the means to define more complete, yet abstract test models. This simplifies validation and improves the readability of test models. The handling of unexpected messages is achieved through the specification of defaults. The concept of defaults is taken from TTCN-3 in which a separate behavior is triggered if an event is observed that is not explicitly handled by the main test case behavior. The partitioning between the main test behavior and the default behavior is up to the designer. Within the testing profile, default behaviors are applied to static behavioral structures. For example, defaults can be applied to combined fragments (within interactions), state machines, states, and regions.

The testing profile concepts used to describe the test behavior can be summarized by

- *Test objective* allowing the designer to express the intention of the test.
- *Test case* is an operation of a test context specifying how a set of cooperating components interact with the SUT to realize a test objective.
- *Default* is a concept for making the behavior description more complete by specifying situations where the described sequence does not happen.
- *Verdict* is a predefined enumeration specifying possible test results, for example, pass, inconclusive, fail, and error.
- *Validation action* is performed by the test component to indicate that the arbiter is informed of the test component's test result.
- *Timers* are used to manipulate and control test behavior as well as to ensure the termination of test cases.
- *Time zones* are used to group components within a distributed system, thereby allowing the comparison of time events within the same time zone.

Another important aspect of test specification is the definition and encoding of test data. For this, the UTP supports wildcards, data pools, data partitions, data selectors, and coding rules. Wildcards are very useful for the handling of unexpected events or events containing many different values. Therefore, the UTP introduces wildcards allowing the specification of (1) any value, denoting any value out of a set of possible values, and (2) any or omitted values, denoting any value or the lack of a value (in the case where multiplicities range from 0 upward).

Figure 2.17 shows a data pool concept (ItemPool), data partitions (ItemPartition and its specializations), and data selector (selectItem) that support the repeated execution of test cases with different data values to stimulate the SUT in various ways. Data pools are associated with test contexts and may include data partitions (equivalence classes) and concrete data values. Data selectors provide different strategies for data selection and data checking. The testing profile also supports the notion of coding rules allowing the user to define the encoding and decoding of test data.

The concepts discussed above provide the capabilities required to construct precise test specifications using UML 2.0. The testing profile includes both

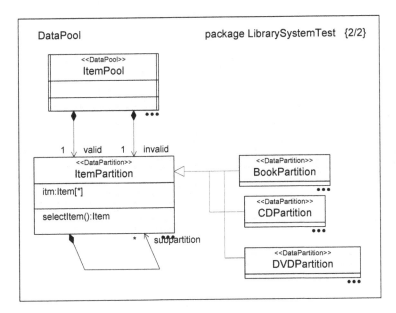

Fig. 2.17. Test data

structural and behavioral elements and provides key domain concepts from testing that make test specification efficient and effective.

In addition to those concepts explained earlier, there are also a few more concepts that are available for advanced purposes:

- *The scheduler* controls test execution and test components. Schedulers are responsible for the creation of test components a synchronized start of the test behavior on the different test components, and for the detection of test case termination.
- *The arbiter* provides a means for evaluating test results derived by different objects within the test system in order to determine an overall verdict for a test case or test context. We refer to this evaluation process as arbitration. Users can either use the default arbitration scheme specified by the profile (i.e. a verdict can only get worse) or define their own arbitration scheme using an arbiter.
- *A test log* provides together with a log action a means to log entries during the test execution for further analysis.
- *A finish action* denotes the completion of the test case behavior of a component, without terminating the component.
- *A determAlt operator* is provided for interactions to specify the deterministic and sequential evaluation of guards of alternative behavior. The determAlt operator always selects the alternative of the first guard, which is fulfilled.

3

Library Example Introduction

Throughout this book, we introduce and explain the concepts and the application of the UML Testing Profile(UTP) by using a simple library system. We choose a library system, because most readers know the basic functionality of a library. Most people have been customers of a library and searched for a book, borrowed a book, and returned a book. As a result, they have an intuitive understanding of the elements managed by such a system. A book may be modeled as a class with attributes such as title, author, status, price, and last borrower. In this chapter, we will briefly introduce the library example including a description of the system structure, its behavior, and the data structures managed by the library system.

3.1 What Is a Library?

A library is an institution that makes items such as books, videos, records, and DVDs. available to borrowers for a limited period of time. The borrowers will return the item to the library after this limited period of time and the item may subsequently be lent to other borrowers. Sometimes the item is not locally available, but may be remotely borrowed from a collaborating library. When an item is acquired from a remote library, the home library acts as a borrower in relation to the remote library.

We summarize the functionality of a Library in a use case diagram as shown in Figure 3.1. This illustrates how the borrower and the librarian are involved in use cases like BorrowItem. The use cases will be formalized with other UML diagrams.

The main concepts are given in the class diagram of Figure 3.3. Our model will mostly apply asynchronous signaling and the signals are defined in Figure 3.4.

The architecture of the library context is given by Figure 3.5. The direct communication between the borrower and the library is meant to describe a

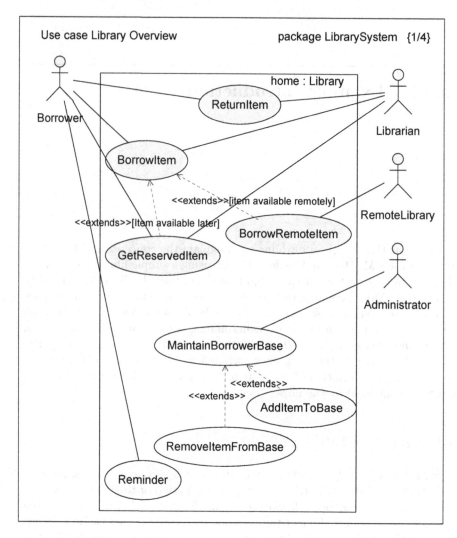

Use case Library Overview   package LibrarySystem {1/4}

Borrower

home : Library

ReturnItem

Librarian

BorrowItem

RemoteLibrary

<<extends>>[item available remotely]

<<extends>>[Item available later]

BorrowRemoteItem

GetReservedItem

Administrator

MaintainBorrowerBase

<<extends>>

<<extends>>

AddItemToBase

RemoveItemFromBase

Reminder

Fig. 3.1. Use case diagram for the Library example

situation where the borrower himself/herself searches on a computer without
the intervention of the librarian.

   The interaction overview diagram in Figure 3.6 presents a formalization of
the BorrowItem use case behavior described in Figure 3.2. In-line interactions
and references to interactions combined by means of flow lines and conditional
branches show the possible flow of control for the BorrowItem use case. Each
flow of control starts in the start node and ends in one of the end nodes. The
interactions referred to in Figure 3.6 are presented in Figures 3.7, 3.8, 3.9,
and 3.12.

us Borrow Item

Borrow Item

Actors: Librarian, Borrower

Preconditions:
The Librarian is logged onto the library management system.

Normal Cases:
1.   The Borrower searches the library system and finds a book
2.1   The book is available now locally: the Borrower asks the Librarian to fetch
      the book and she does so
      -OR-
2.2   The book will be available locally later: the Borrower may decide to reserve
      the book by mailing the Librarian and she will do the actual reservation
      -OR-
2.3   The book is not available locally: the Librarian will query whether the book
      is available at a remote library.
      2.3.1   If book is available remotely, reserve if the Borrower desires.
      2.3.2   If the book is not available remotely either, no loan is finalized.

Exceptional Cases:
  E1.   The Borrower's library card is invalid. The Librarian informs the Borrower.
        If the Borrower desires, she may be issued a new card by running the Add
        User use case.

  E2.   The Borrower owes fines for overdue books. The Librarian informs the
        Borrower, who may pay the fine.

  E3.   The borrower has checked out the maximum number of books allows.
        The Librarian informs the Borrower, who may reserve the book or return a
        book or quit.

Fig. 3.2. Borrow Item use case

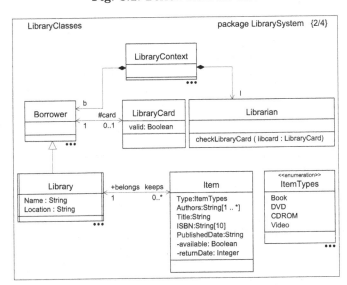

Fig. 3.3. Classes of the Library

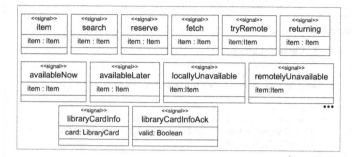

Fig. 3.4. Signals of the Library

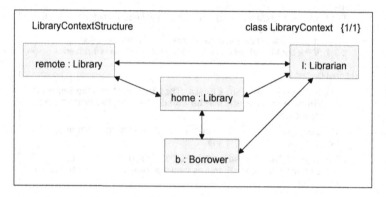

Fig. 3.5. The composite structure of the Library context

A comparison of Figure 3.6 with Figure 3.2 shows the correspondence of the representation. The flow of control through the first branch marked available now corresponds to the flow described by the items 1 and 2.1 in Figure 3.2. The flow of control through the available later branch reflects the flow through the items 1 and 2.2. The remaining three flows of control in Figure 3.6 cover the case where an item is requested from the remote library. The two flows of control that end in the states ItemAvailableLater and ItemUnavailable refer to the flows that end in item 2.3.1 and 2.3.2 in Figure 3.2. The third flow that ends in ItemBorrowed describes the situation where an item, which is available locally, is owned by the remote library.

Let us describe the different scenarios in more detail. All borrowing scenarios start with a search for the item to be borrowed (see the first referenced interaction in Figure 3.6).

If the item is available (Figure 3.7), the borrower has to authenticate and can fetch the item from the librarian. The authentication procedure, referenced in Figure 3.7, is shown in Figure 3.11.

If the item is unavailable (but owned by the library), Figure 3.8 describes the behavior of the library user. Notice that the authentication and remote borrowing are both optional, as the user may decide not to wait to borrow the book.

One complex behavior of this use case is the situation, where an item is requested from a remote library. This is described separately by the BorrowItemNonlocally (which references BorrowRemoteItem) interaction referenced in Figure 3.6 and shown in Figure 3.9.

BorrowRemoteItem in Figure 3.10 includes an alt statement, describing the two alternative behaviors described by this interaction. The first alternative describes the case where the item is available. It ends in a situation where the item is reserved and will arrive at the local library later. The second alternative describes the situation where the item cannot be borrowed remotely. The BorrowRemoteItem interaction in Figure 3.10 also includes optional behavior that describes that the Borrower may decide to reserve an item after he has been informed that the item is only available later.

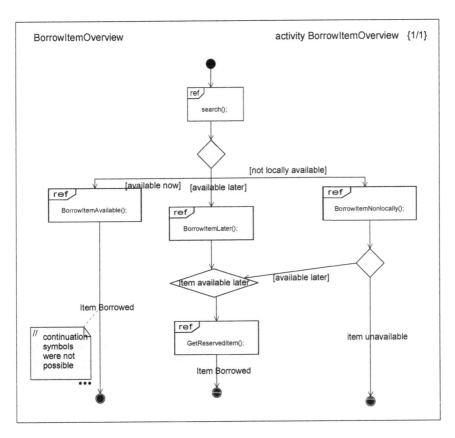

Fig. 3.6. Borrowing an item

The three different sub-behaviors of BorrowItemOverview are shown in Figures 3.7, 3.8, and 3.9. They will give rise to individual test cases.

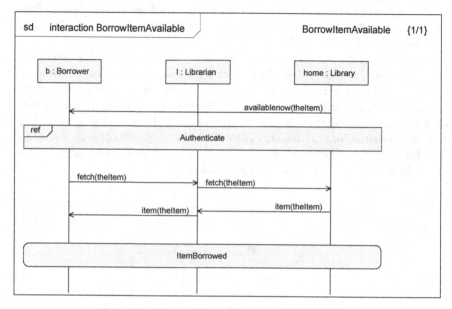

Fig. 3.7. Borrow Item that is available locally

Figure 3.6 illustrates that the borrower need not authenticate himself until he is about to borrow the book. This is because authentication is located in the interactions (Figures 3.7, 3.8, and 3.9) which are the possibilities referenced after a search. Searching itself does not require authentication.

In Figure 3.8, the opt construct defines that the borrower may decide not to reserve the book at all since it was not readily available. Similarly, in Figure 3.9, the opt construct is used to indicate that the borrower may decide not to borrow the book if it is only available from a remote library. Again the borrower may decide not to borrow because the book is not locally available. Otherwise authentication is needed before the BorrowRemoteItem behavior (Figure 3.10) occurs. The BorrowRemoteItem situation corresponds to use case 2.3 in Figure 3.2. The book is not available locally and the Librarian searches remotely. Whether the remote library has the book available directly or later is of less importance as the Borrower must wait for the physical transfer anyway and the Borrower is told that the item will be available later. He may then choose to reserve the item, and sooner or later the item will be transferred from the remote library to the home library. Then the Borrower can pick it up according to the scenario shown in Figure 3.12. This corresponds to use case 2.3.1 in Figure 3.2. If the book is not available at the remote library either,

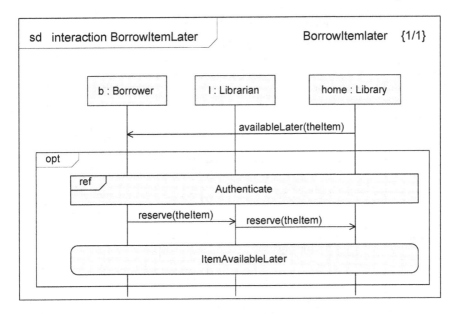

Fig. 3.8. Borrow item later knowing that the book will be available at the local library later

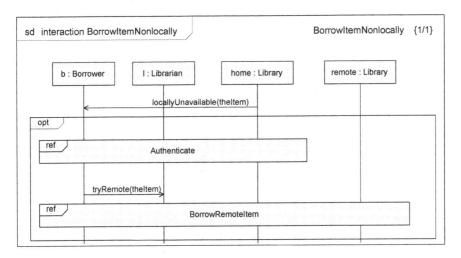

Fig. 3.9. Borrow item that is not locally available

then the book is considered unavailable, and this information is given to the Borrower corresponding to use case 2.3.2 in Figure 3.2.

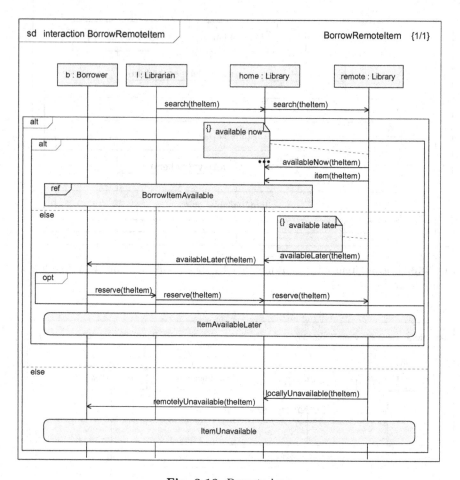

Fig. 3.10. Remote loan

The use case description in Figure 3.2 structures the behavior into normal and exceptional behavior. The exceptional cases are all related to abnormal outcomes of the authentication procedure which is required for the reservation and retrieval of items. For example, Figure 3.8 presents the BorrowItemLater interaction (also referenced in Figure 3.6) which refers to the interaction Authenticate. The normal authentication scenario is shown in Figure 3.11. It would also be possible to include the exceptional cases in this diagram, but separate diagrams for different cases improve the readability. Therefore, we have chosen here to show only the normal authentication situation where the library card is ok and no restrictions are placed upon the bearer before executing his/her current requests.

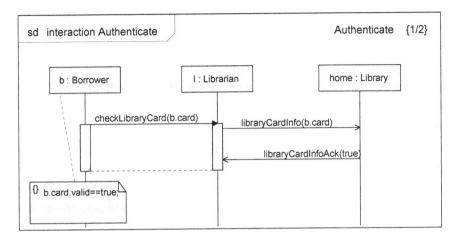

Fig. 3.11. Simple authentication of library card

For completeness, we also give in Figure 3.12 the GetReservedItem situation.

3.2 What Is Inside a Library?

We have introduced the concept of a library from the standpoint of a borrower, an outside person who visits this kind of institution and takes advantage of its services.

The computer scientist or system designer who is going to construct the supporting computerized system for the library will also have to consider the constituents of the library information system. The construction of a library system is not in itself our task in this book, but it is important to point out that the library system has constituents and eventually that these constituents may be tested separately or in combination with others to form the whole system.

One approach to modeling the library is to look at what we may find inside the institution. We find the physical items that are to be lent to the borrowers. We also find search terminals that the borrowers can use. We may also find means for security, for example, a gate that controls unauthorized removal of items. Furthermore, we have the librarian's unit that is used for registration of loans and returns. We describe this understanding of the insides of a Library in Figure 3.13. This description is not meant to form the basis of a serious implementation, but rather to serve as the foundation for explaining different

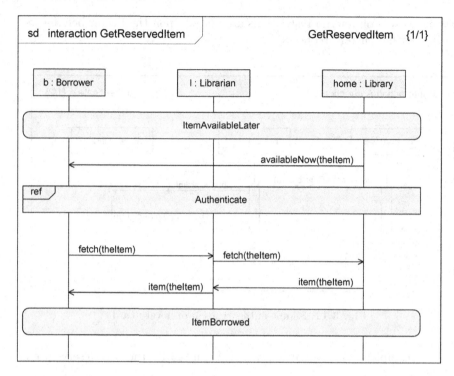

Fig. 3.12. GetReservedItem after the item has become available

kinds of testing. This again emphasizes the important point in modeling that we model only what we find relevant. Thus, there may be many real items in a library that we do not model, such as green plants and even the book shelves.

3.3 Testing a Library

In the rest of this book, we shall go in some detail into the testing of this Library. We shall give examples of testing the insides of the library as well as testing the library as a whole. We hope the library example will be both intuitive for the reader and complex enough to illustrate the mechanisms of the UTP.

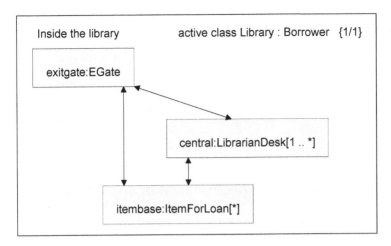

Fig. 3.13. The composite structure of the Library itself

Part II

Functional Testing

Overview

Functional testing is testing against the functional requirements of the SUT. It focuses mainly on the outputs generated by the SUT in response to selected, inputs and execution conditions. Functional testing is *black-box testing* and, therefore, both terms are often used as synonyms in literature. UML-based testing of nonfunctional requirements, such as real time and performance testing, will be presented in Part III of this book.

UML is a specification language and allows functional requirements to be specified using UML diagrams. For example, the scenarios described in use cases directly corresponds to a set of test cases targeting a common functional capability. Sequence diagrams, often provided as refinement of use case behavior, can be seen as abstract test cases. Further structural information in UML diagrams, such as state charts defining the behavior of a class, may also be used to identify test cases for functional testing.

Black-box testing approaches can be used to define tests for all levels of testing in the V- and W-model (Figures 1.1 and 1.2. We will therefore describe the use of the UML testing profile for Unit Level Testing (Chapter 4), for Component and Integration Level Testing (Chapter 5), and for System and Acceptance Level Testing (Chapter 6).

We would like to mention that glass-box and grey-box testing approaches are domains for Unit, Component, and Integration Level Testing. Glass-box and grey-box testing requires knowledge about implementation details to define coverage criteria for the implementation or communication details among implementation entities.

This book only deals with black-box testing approaches because we base the test specification on UML models and not on implementations. However, some principles of these kinds of testing approaches can be applied to UML models to assist in the identification of test cases.

4

Unit Level Testing

Unit level testing is used to verify the behavior of a single unit within a program. Herein, the unit which should be tested must be isolated from other units within the system in order to prevent interference of test results. In object-oriented programming, a single unit is typically a class or operation defined within a class. Typical programming errors which can be discovered during unit level tests include division by zero, wrong path setting, or incorrect pointer settings.

Black-box testing can be applied for all levels of testing. They only differ in the kind of *System Under Test* (SUT) they address. While component and integration testing is performed on several units of a system working together, and system testing refers to the whole system, unit level testing is performed on individual units within the system. In this chapter, we discuss the concerns of unit level testing, including how to use the UTP for unit level test specifications. The use of the profile is illustrated by means of the library example.

4.1 UTP and Unit Level Testing

Unit level tests can be derived from UML models. A unit in a UML model might be a single class or an operation. Black-box test is performed without the knowledge of the internal structure of the SUT. Thus, the prerequisite to unit testing the SUT using UML is that the tester must get access by calling public operations or by sending signals via an interface.

☞**Tip 1** Unit level test scope

For unit level testing, an SUT is an individual unit (e.g., a class or an operation) which is to be tested.

⚓ UTP Concept 1 SUT

SUT stands for system under test. For unit level testing, the SUT is an object or an operation which can be tested by calling operations or sending signals via public interfaces.

Before defining a test suite in UML, a new package for unit level testing needs to be created, and the system model must be imported to the test package in order to get access to the SUT. Figure 4.1 illustrates the package dependencies of the TTDTestingProfile package with predefined UTP concepts, the system model package LibrarySystem of the Library Example and its newly created test package LibraryUnitTest. The test model imports the system model in order to get access to the SUT during testing. To enable test specification, the test model needs import of the UTP concept package.

UTP Methodology Rule 1 Creating UTP test model

1. Create a new UML package for the unit level test.
2. Import the SUT system model package.
3. Import the package where UTP concepts are defined.

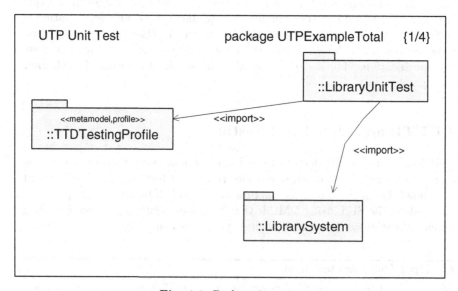

Fig. 4.1. Package imports

When using UTP, tests are performed within a given contex. This context is where test cases are defined, as well as the test configuration and related concepts. In a unit level UTP model, a test context is a stereotyped class which contains the unit level test cases as operations. In order to create a test context within the UTP model, a new UML class needs to be created and the UTP test context stereotype must be applied to the class.

⚓**UTP Concept 2** Test context

The test context is a stereotyped class that contains the test cases (as operations) and whose composite structure defines the test configuration. The classifier behavior of the test context provides the test control, which determines the order of execution of test cases.

UTP Methodology Rule 2 Define test context in a UTP test model.

To create a test context class for a unit level test, the following steps are needed:

1. *Define a test context class with stereotype <<Test Context>>.*
2. *List all the test cases as public operations in the test context class.*

Figure 4.2 shows the test context definition for the Library example. Inside Package LibraryUnitTest, a test context class called LibraryUnitTestContext is created and assigned with stereotype <<TestContext>>. This test context

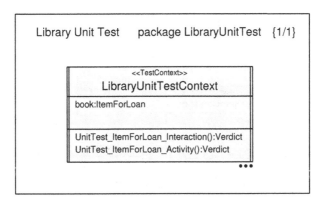

Fig. 4.2. Test context

class owns an attribute called book of class ItemForLoan and defines two test cases called UnitTest_ItemForLoan_Interaction() and UnitTest_ItemForLoan_ Activity(). The concrete behavior specification of those two test cases are shown in other diagrams later in this chapter. Both test cases are public operations returning test verdicts as results.

As the names of the test cases already indicate, our unit level tests are performed on library items for loan. These operate on the concrete system specification related to the library items. These are part of the specification of the library system itself.

The concrete classes and signals that are part of the library system are available to the unit test package as they have been imported from the LibrarySystem package. Figure 4.3 shows the class and signal definitions of the library system. For our unit level testing example, the class ItemForLoan is the class to be tested. An Item in a library can be a Book, CD, DVD, or Video. It has several attributes, including one or more authors, a title, an ISBN number, and a publishing date. The ItemForLoan class represents an item that can be loaned to a library user. It adds the perspective that an item can be in either a good or a bad condition. If an item is in a bad condition, it needs to

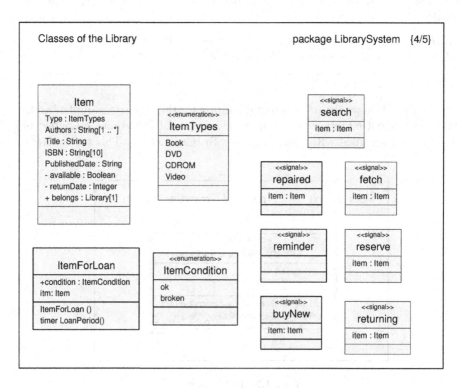

Fig. 4.3. Classes and signals in the Library System

be repaired before handed out again to another borrower. The signals shown in Figure 4.3 illustrate the ways that a tester can trigger various behaviors on the SUT.

4.1.1 State Machines

In order to generate test cases for the SUT ItemForLoan, we need a complete behavioral specification of the SUT class. UML state machines are the standard way to describe the behavior of a class.

☞ Tip 2 State machine adequacy

In order to derive useful test cases, the class behavior must be described. State machines provide good means for class behavior description. Test cases can be generated from the state machine specification, and the more precise and complete the state machines are, the better the derived test cases.

In our library example, class ItemForLoan is to be tested. Figure 4.4 illustrates its behavior specification by a State Machine. An ItemForLoan can exist in various states. In its initial state, it is available to any borrower. After it has been borrowed by a certain library user, it may be returned back in a good or broken condition. In latter case, the item will be repaired (toBeRepaired). In case that the item is still borrowed, but requested by another user, the item will be reserved for that user. When a reserved item is returned, depending on the condition of the item, it will be repaired (repairForReserver or availableFor-Reserver). If it is available for the reserver, the reserver gets the item as soon as it is returned, and the item moves into the borrowed state. In cases where a broken item cannot be repaired, it will be replaced by a new version of the item.

4.1.2 Interactions

In UTP, a test scenario is described informally by a test objective, which is simply the textual description of the purpose of a test case. Test cases are the concrete realization of a set of behaviors which achieve the test objective. When using state machines for behavioral specification, test cases can be generated by simulating the behavior of the state machine. This simulation seeks to achieve a given coverage criteria (e.g., transition coverage, state coverage) [2] by ensuring that test data values are used to trigger the SUT in a way that helps achieve the coverage criteria.

In the library example, one test objective may be to *"verify that a broken item returned to the library is sent for repair."* To achieve this objective, concrete test cases with message flow between the SUT and the test system are created. This can be done using UML interaction diagrams or activity

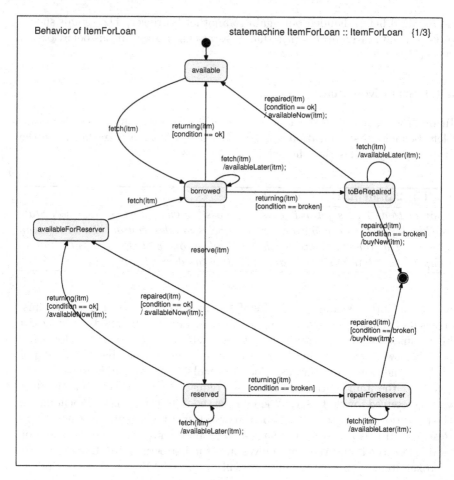

Fig. 4.4. State machine of item

⚓ **UTP Concept 3** Test objective

A test objective describes the purpose of the test in an informal way.

---

diagrams to show communication between the test system and the SUT. For unit level test cases in a UTP model, the test context instance represents the test system.

Depending on predefined test strategies and coverage criteria (e.g., statement, branch, path, or other coverage criteria), the state machine of ItemForLoan can be simulated and the graph can be traversed in order to derive the test cases. In this example, we utilized *state coverage criteria*, which seeks to reach all of the states in the ItemForLoan state machine (Figure 4.4) at least

---

UTP Methodology Rule 3 Specifying test cases with interaction diagrams

For a unit-level test case, the test context instance can be used to trigger the SUT. Interaction diagrams provide good means for detailed test behavior specification. This is done using the following steps:

1. *Define a test case by creating a new interaction diagram.*
2. *Initiate the test case with an instance of the test context.*
3. *The test context instance creates the SUT instances and triggers it using operation calls or signals.*
4. *The order of these calls/signals is derived from the system model by simulation with an appropriate coverage criterion.*
5. *At the end of the test case, set the unit level testing verdict by returning a verdict value. For system derived test cases, this is typically* pass.

---

once. A single test case is enough to achieve this coverage criterion. Figure 4.5 shows the derived unit level test case called UnitTest_ItemForLoan_Interaction in an interaction diagram.

⏚ **UTP Concept 4** Test case

A UTP test case concretizes a test objective by triggering inputs and observing outputs of the system. A test case always returns a test verdict.

The diagram shows in the beginning the test context instance TestLibrary-TestContext, which creates a new instance called book of class ItemForLoan. The item is available and will be fetched by the user. In its borrowed state, it can be reserved by a further user and when the first borrower returns the item in a broken condition, it gets repaired for and borrowed to the reserver. When the reserver returns the item in an irreparable condition, the item is replaced by a new exemplar. If this test case terminates successfully, all states of the ItemForLoan object will have been covered.

A test must deliver its result in a certain form to the external world. In UTP, they are in the form of test verdicts. Predefined verdicts in UTP include *pass, fail, inconclusive, and* error. The *pass verdict indicates that the SUT behaves correctly for the specified test behavior. The* fail verdict describes that the SUT does not behave according to the behavior. The *inconclusive verdict is used when the test neither passes nor fails, but is still valid according to the specification of the SUT. Finally, the* error verdict indicates an issue within the test system itself.

Test cases generated automatically from the system specification typically represent the expected correct behavior of the system. Thus, the test results

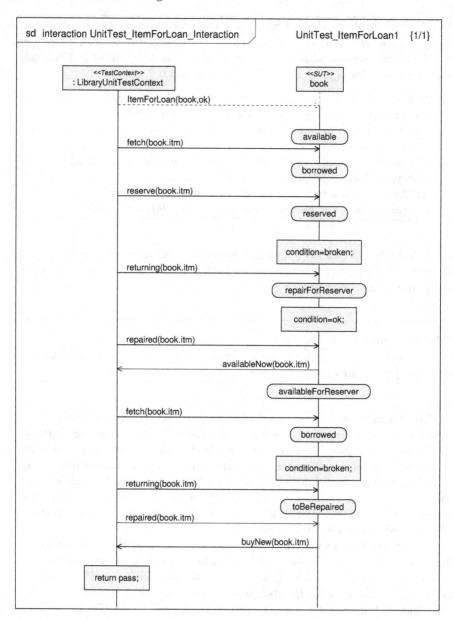

Fig. 4.5. Test case—interaction diagram

are usually set to *pass* at the end of these test cases. Accordingly, the verdict of test case UnitTest_ItemForLoan_Interaction in our library example is assigned to pass.

⇩**UTP Concept 5** Test verdicts

In UTP, each test case returns a verdict. Predefined verdicts are pass, fail, inconclusive, *and* error.

4.1.3 Activity Diagrams

Test cases can also be illustrated by UML activity diagrams. Activity diagrams provide a slightly different view of the system behavior than interaction diagrams. While the latter concentrates on the communication between the objects, an activity diagrams lays its focus more on the local behavior of an object.

Figure 4.6 shows a test case for the Library Example in an activity diagram, also derived from the state machine introduced in Figure 4.4. Here, the operation calls and message exchanges between the objects are not in the focus. Instead, the internal activities of each of the objects are illustrated.

UTP Methodology Rule 4 Specifying test cases with activity diagrams

For a unit-level test case, the test context instance can be used in order to trigger the SUT. Activity diagrams provide good means for detailed test behavior specification. To do so, the following steps are needed:

1. *Define a test case by creating a new activity diagram.*
2. *Initiate the test case with a test context instance by creating a partition for the test context in the activity diagram.*
3. *Parallely to test context, a partition for the SUT instance is needed.*
4. *Derive test behavior from the system model by simulation and applying coverage criteria.*
5. *At the end of the test case, set the unit level testing verdict by returning a verdict value. For test cases derived from the system specification, this is usually the* pass *value.*

Two partitions called LibraryUnitTestContext and ItemForLoan and their activity flows are shown in Figure 4.6. The transitions and state information in the state machine of ItemForLoan are transformed to activities in the diagram. Within the ItemForLoan partition, the availability of the library item is checked. Depending on its status, two different activity flows are traversed. In

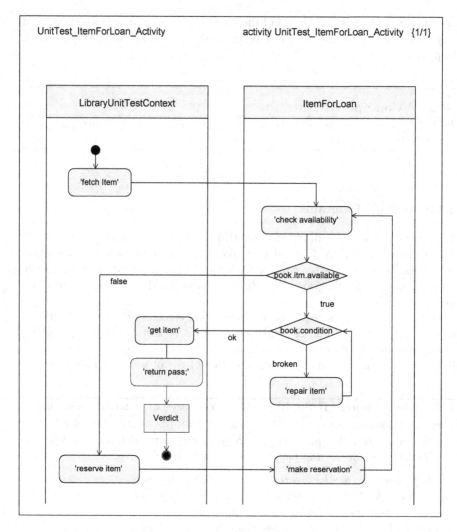

Fig. 4.6. Test case—activity diagram

this test case, the end of the activity diagram can only be reached if the book is in a good status and is available to another borrower. In this case, the test result will be set to pass.

4.2 Chapter Summary

In this chapter, we introduced several key UTP concepts, including SUT, test context, test cases, and predefined UTP test verdicts. These concepts can be used to model unit level tests (as well as other types of tests). We use state machines as a basis for modeling the behavior of the SUT. We then illustrate how state machines can be simulated to allow the derivation of test cases. These are generated by traversing the graph using user-defined test strategies and coverage criteria. The test cases are modeled using behavior diagrams such as interaction diagrams (for focusing on communication between objects) or activity diagrams (for focusing on the local activity of the objects in the test case).

5

Component and Integration Level Testing

As described in Chapter 4, a software unit is the smallest separately testable element in the design of a software system. They cannot be subdivided into other components. A software component is composed of software units. It is a system element offering a predefined service and is able to communicate with other software components. Software components may be tested in isolation or in combination with other components. The former is called *component level testing*, whereas the latter refers to *integration level testing*. Integration level testing is the phase of software testing in which software components are combined and tested as a group.

During the development of complex software systems, software components are often in different development states. Whereas one component may be in its implementation phase, another component may be ready for integration with other components. Different development states cannot be avoided. They are the consequence of parallel development in several groups of developers, different size and complexities of the software components and project priorities.

Component and integration level testing is therefore often confronted with the problem that the service provided by the component or a group of components under test (the SUT) requires functionality of components which are not ready for integration. Delays of the component and integration level testing process can be avoided by the development of emulators for the missing functionality and an elaborated project plan which considers the integration order of the components.

Due to the similarities of component and integration level testing, we cover both in this chapter. To ease the reading, we will mainly use the term *integration level testing*. Only where necessary, we will refer to *component level testing*.

In this chapter, we will discuss some basics on integration level testing and show how the UML Testing Profile (UTP) can be utilized for this kind of testing.

5.1 Integration Strategies and Integration Level Testing

The objective of integration level testing is to test the smooth interoperation of components. Some properties may be tested statically, whereas errors related to the semantics of the communication can only be tested dynamically. For example, a compiler can statically check the correct usage of interfaces provided by a component, whereas the exchange of syntactically correct but semantically incorrect information can only be detected dynamically.

Integration level testing depends heavily on the integration strategy used for assembling the whole system. Well-known integration strategies are *big-bang*, *bottom-up*, *top-down*, and *adhoc integration*:

- The integration of the whole system in onestep is called *big-bang integration*. In this case, integration level testing starts after the finalization of all components. The problems with this approach are that the integration level testing starts very late in the development process and that all the integration problems appear at once. Testing may become complicated, and it can be very difficult to identify the source of errors observed during the test.
- A *bottom-up integration* strategy requires a hierarchical system structure. Software components with basic functionality are assembled to yield more complex components, which are integrated to produce even more complex subsystems, etc., until the complete system is produced. Testing is done in all steps of integration. The advantage of this strategy is that only test drivers, but no emulators, are needed for testing because the availability of already tested lower-level components is a prerequisite for the integration of the next level of hierarchy. The problem with this strategy is that the test of the overall functionality of the system starts very late, and therefore, design and efficiency problems related to the basic functions of the system may be detected only at the end of the integration level testing.
- *Top-down integration* also requires a hierarchical system structure. It is the opposite of bottom-up integration. Integration starts from the top, and step by step lower-level functionality is added until the complete system is realized. For integration level testing, the main disadvantage of this strategy is that the lower-level functionality is not available and has to be emulated. This is normally done by implementing emulators for the missing components.
- Bottom-up integration and top-down integration require a hierarchical systemk structure and predictable finalization dates for the different components. In most cases, these prerequisites cannot be guaranteed. Therefore, the most popular integration strategy is *adhoc integration*, that is, components are integrated whenever they are finalized and whenever it is reasonable. Integration testing with an adhoc integration strategy also requires the emulation of missing functionality.

Several integration strategies require emulators for missing functionality. These emulators belong to the test configuration, which will be explained in the next section.

5.2 Test Configuration, Test Components, and Emulators

Test configurations are needed for all kinds of testing and are therefore not unique to integration level testing. However, due to the emulators mentioned in the previous section, test configurations for integration level testing are often more comprehensive than for other kinds of testing. Therefore, we introduce the UTP concept of *test configuration* (UTP concept 6) in this section. The definition of test configuration refers to the UTP concept *test component* (UTP concept 7).

⥥ **UTP Concept 6** Test configuration

A *test configuration* is the collection of test component objects with connections between the test component objects and from test component objects to the SUT. The test configuration defines both (1) test component objects and connections when a test case is started (the initial test configuration) and (2) the maximal number of test component objects and connections during the test execution.

⥥ **UTP Concept 7** Test component

A *test component* is a class of a test system. Test component objects realize the behavior of a test case. A test component has a set of interfaces via which it may communicate via connections with other test components or with the SUT.

Test components are understood as classes which play the role of users of the SUT, that is, they test the capabilities provided by the SUT. They drive the test and calculate an overall test verdict. Driving the test means that test component instances stimulate the SUT and observe the responses from the SUT.

A further class of objects in integration level testing are emulators, which have already been mentioned in the previous section. Emulators simulate missing functionality which is needed by the SUT to provide its service. They differ from test components, in that they do not provide information that is used to set the verdict of the test case. For testing, we can distinguish three kinds of emulators:

- *Dummies* are very rudimentary implementations of missing functionality. Often they only provide interfaces definitions such as function headers, which are necessary to compile the subsystem without errors.
- *Stubs* provide enough functionality for testing. A stub may be implemented for a certain set of tests and react for these tests in a reasonable manner.
- *Mock Objects* have more intelligence than dummies and stubs. They may be complete simulators of the missing functionality.

Emulators can be seen as utilities of a test configuration. Therefore, they should be defined as UML *utilities*. Emulators and, if necessary, different kinds of emulators can be distinguished from other objects by using a name prefix (Methodology Rule 5).

UTP Methodology Rule 5 Definition of emulators

Emulators such as dummies, stubs, and mock objects should be defined as utilities in a test configuration for component and integration level testing. Name prefixes like emulator_ (for emulators in general), dummy_, stub_, or mock_ can be used to distinguish emulators from other kinds of utilities.

5.3 UTP and Integration Level Testing

Similar to unit level testing (Section 4.1), we start the specification of an integration level test for our library example with the definition of the new package Library Integration Test (Figure 5.1) which imports the UML model of the library system and the UTP (the imports are not shown in Figure 5.1).

For defining an integration level test for our library example, we have to first identify the components which are integrated into the SUT, the test components driving the test and utilities emulating missing functionality. As an example, consider a situation close to finalization of the library system, where the functionality of remote loans is only implemented for the home library, but not for the remote side. In order to test this functionality, the SUT is defined by the home library; we have two test components playing the roles of borrower and librarian and a utility emulating the needed functionality of the remote library. These objects and the relations among them are shown in the test context in Figure 5.2. The definitions of test context and the test components are shown in Figure 5.1. Both test components inherit properties from the corresponding objects in the library system.

The utility Mock_remote (Figure Test Context for Integration Level Testing) is a mock object. It is considered to be an instantiation of the library class of the library system. If the behaviour of the Library class is defined very

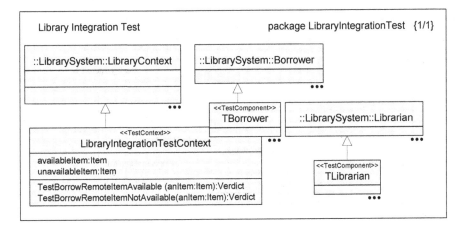

Fig. 5.1. Package LibraryIntegrationTest

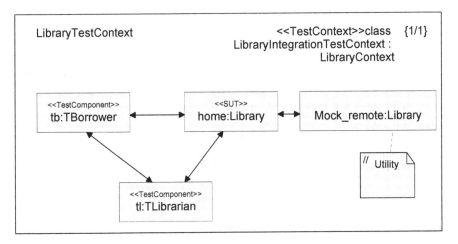

Fig. 5.2. Test context for integration level testing

precisely, it may be possible to generate the code of the mock object automatically from its specification. Emulators with less intelligence, that is, dummies and stubs, maybe generated directly from the test specification (Tip 3).

☞**Tip 3** Generation of emulator objects

Code generation and simulation facilities of UML tools may be used to generate emulator objects for integration and component level testing automatically. Intelligent emulators, that is, mock objects, may be generated from the UML system specification. Less intelligent emulators, that is, dummies and stubs, may be derived directly from the test specification.

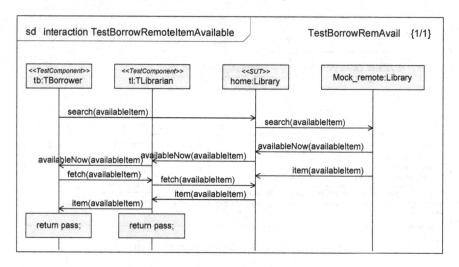

Fig. 5.3. Test case TestBorrowRemoteItemAvailable

The LibraryIntegrationTestContext class (Figure 5.1) includes the two test cases TestBorrowRemoteItemAvailable and TestBorrowRemoteItemNotAvailable. The test behaviors of these test cases are described by the sequence diagrams shown in Figures 5.3 and 5.4. A comparison with Figure 3.10 explains the source of both test behaviors. They describe two possible scenarios when trying to borrow an item remotely. Thus, they are an adaptation of behaviors defined in the UML system specification of the library.

The example test cases show the possibility of deriving tests for component and integration level testing from UML system and component specifications. Such test cases focus on testing the functionality of the system, but not on

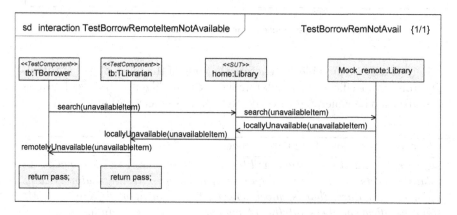

Fig. 5.4. Test case TestBorrowRemoteItemNotAvailable

complex communication patterns among components or potential bottlenecks. Therefore, it is advisable to also develop integration test cases that go beyond the behavior described in the system specification.

5.4 Chapter Summary

In this chapter, we introduced the UTP concepts of *test components* and *test configuration*. Furthermore, we explained the main principles of component and integration level testing and described how the UTP supports this kind of testing. The main peculiarity of component and integration level testing is the need of emulators to simulate missing functionality during the testing process. Emulators should be modeled as UML utilities and may be generated automatically from UML models. Test cases for component and integration level testing may be derived from functional requirements in the form of UML diagrams. Additionally defined test cases should also be provided and should focus on implementation aspects of the SUT.

6

System and Acceptance Level Testing

The goal of system level testing is to verify that the system under test conforms to its requirements. Acceptance testing is basically an extension of system testing in which requirements and the test cases associated with validating them are developed by or with the customer(s) and are considered to be contractual descriptions of the required system behavior. In doing both system and acceptance testing, we would like to produce a set of tests that exhaustively check all of the normal and exceptional behaviors of the system, which are specified by complete and correct requirements. *Completeness* means that we are satisfied that sufficient aspects of our system behavior have been specified. *Correctness* means that there are no ambiguities, errors, or inconsistencies within the requirements specification. If the system under test passes all of the tests derived from the requirements, then we have a high degree of confidence that the system fulfills its requirements.

In most real-world systems, we are faced with the challenge that the requirements cover an extremely large or even infinite set of possible behaviors, which cannot be tested due to time and funding constraints. Therefore, we typically define criteria that guide us in determining what and how many tests are needed to achieve adequate testing (e.g., coverage criteria, software reliability criteria [18, 19]).

Another issue is that requirements are often incomplete and change during the system life cycle. Incompleteness is often a result of under-specification (e.g., the requirements may not cover all possible exceptional cases). In order to cope with such problems, we have to ensure the consistency between requirements and tests (e.g., by automatic consistency checks) and conduct other types of testing throughout the system life cycle (e.g., field testing and regression testing). Testing is essentially a sampling problem, and we are trying to find the most efficient sample of behaviors that will validate that the system satisfies its requirements.

To help with completeness, correctness, and consistency in our methodology, we promote the notion of constructing UML specifications to represent the requirements wherever this is possible.[1] This leads toward a more precise understanding of the system and of what is meant by the requirements. Following this approach, we can obtain a number of benefits:

- The use of graphical specification techniques makes it easier to communicate about the requirements, thereby improving their validation.
- The action of constructing rigorous requirements forces the user to think about a more comprehensive set of possible system behaviors leading to a more complete requirements specification.
- More rigorous requirement models allow the early introduction of testing, that is, automated analysis tools that can discover errors and ambiguities within the specification. Furthermore, simulation tools that enable the requirements to be executed may provide feedback during the requirements construction.
- Parts of the requirements can be reused during the construction of test specifications, thereby ensuring better consistency between tests and requirements.

The precision and completeness of the requirements directly affect the effectiveness of the test cases derived from the requirements. Thus, developing precise and complete requirements is a necessity for good system and acceptance level testing.

6.1 UTP and System Level Testing

The basis of our methodology for applying the UML Testing Profile (UTP) to system level testing is to reuse existing UML specifications representing requirements on the overall system. These may include

- use cases produced to capture the main functions of the system,
- activity diagrams describing workflow or business processes,
- class and object diagrams specifying the domain model or the system structure,
- interactions describing the communication among the different objects, and
- state machines defining the dynamic behavior of objects.

Since the use of activity diagrams, class diagrams, and state machines for testing is discussed in Chapters 4 and 5, and the use of these diagrams for system level testing is comparable to their use for component and integration level testing, we will concentrate in this section on use case diagrams and interactions. In our methodology, interactions are seen as concretizations and formalizations of use cases.

---

[1] Some requirements may not be describable with UML such as robustness requirements. Such requirements have to be specified by means of other notations or languages.

6.1.1 Use Cases

Use cases are specifications that describe the functional capabilities of the system and their relation to the stakeholders. In UML, use cases are diagrammatic only. The standard provides no guidance for capturing the content of use cases in a formal or textual form. In spite of this, use cases can serve as a valuable basis for identifying the test cases that cover the expected user capabilities. Figure 3.1 shows a use case diagram for the Library example. Figure 3.6 provides a textual description of the *BorrowItem* use case. In the following examples, the *BorrowItem* use case will be utilized to discuss the derivation of system level test cases.

☞ **Tip 4** Use case adequacy

The better the use case, the better the test coverage achieved. So it is good practice to ensure that use cases cover all involved system actors, preconditions, as well as cover both normal and exceptional situations.

The textual description in Figure 3.6 highlights the specific aspects of the behavior associated with the use case. It lists the actors, names, and the preconditions and divides the behavior into normal and exceptional cases. The normal and the exceptional cases may have variants and alternatives. Figure 3.6 includes some variants for the normal cases of the *BorrowItem* use case. For example, the items 2.3.1 and 2.3.2 describe variants for the interaction with a remote library, if a book is not locally available.

Test artifacts derived from use cases

The use cases and the corresponding textual descriptions identify the main system level test cases and provide a natural tree-like structure of the test context for system level testing. For our Library example, this structure is shown in Figure 6.1. The root of the tree is the test context itself.

☞ **Tip 5** Testing scope

The use case sets the scope for the UTP test context. The use case subject typically represents the system under test and the actors represent the test components.

The nodes and the leaves represent test cases. The tree nodes divide test cases into groups and subgroups. The test case descriptions related to the nodes may call the test case descriptions of the lower levels.

For example, for a complete test of the BorrowItem use case, the test case *TC_BorrowItem* (see Figure 6.1) must call the test cases that test the

normal and the exceptional behavior, that is, *TC_ BorrowItem_ Normal* and
TC_ BorrowItem_ Exceptional. The leaves of tree structure are test cases that
represent flows of control in the use case descriptions. For example, the test
case *TestBorrowLocallyAvailable* in Figure 6.1 may test the flow of control
described by the line numbers 1 and 1.1 in Figure 3.6.

UTP Methodology Rule 6 Use cases to tests

---

*Use cases can provide a natural tree-like structure for the system level test
context; where nodes and leaves in the structure represent test cases. The
paths through the tree represent the control flow for the test context. Hence,
the recommended process flow for deriving tests from system requirements is*

1. *Develop adequate use cases*
2. *Determine the UTP test context from use cases*
3. *Formalize use cases using interactions*
4. *Map interactions to UTP test specifications*

The structure of a test context obtained by use case analysis can be represented by using Testing Profile means. As shown in Figure 6.2, the test
cases for the system level test of our library example are contained in the test

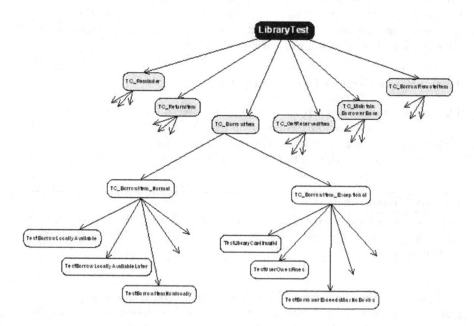

Fig. 6.1. Tree-like structure of the test context

<<TestContext>> **LibrarySystemTestContext**
theItem: Item dp:ItemPool
TC_Reminder () : Verdict TestBorrowLocallyAvailable (Param1 : Item) : Verdict DataDrivenTestCase () : Verdict TestBorrowLocallyAvailableLater () : Verdict TestBulkItemSearch(P1 : ItemPool, P2 : Integer) : Verdict

Fig. 6.2. Test suite structure based on use cases

context *LibraryTestContext*. This test context acts as a root for our hierarchical test structure. The test cases listed in the test context include both the test cases shown in Figure 6.1 and other test cases not present in that diagram.

Test artifacts derived from interactions

We now discuss how to derive UTP test artifacts from interactions that describe the system being tested. This is a detailed expansion of step 4 from Methodology Rule 6.

UTP Methodology Rule 7 Interactions to UTP test specification

The following five steps are useful for developing test cases from interactions:

1. *Determine the test architecture and test components. This includes the test context and key system under test classes which are imported into the architecture.*
2. *Select a scenario from the use case to realize. A scenario is a specific path through the use case.*
3. *Explore the interactions defined for the selected scenario.*
4. *Use the test components to derive a test interaction for the required scenario. This is done by replacing key instances in the interactions from step 3 with test components. Test components are classifiers used to derive the test cases. The test component instances provide stimuli for the system under test and receive observations from the system.*
5. *Apply timers and verdicts to the test interaction. Verdicts are based on the observations of the test components. The collective verdicts from all test components involved in a test case will together form the overall verdict of the test case. Define default behaviors for the test cases.*

Step 1 and Step 2. We select the *BorrowItem* use case as the basis for our example test case derivation. This use case is illustrated in Figures 3.5 and 3.6, and the library system forms one part of the test context. As actors for this use, case we choose a librarian and a borrower. These will define the test components. Since not much more than the concept name of the librarian and the borrower is known from the Library model, we must add properties of these concepts in our test specification. We must define how they will stimulate the library system and how they will judge the observations.

The package containing the test context for our library example is given in Figure 6.3. The package imports the Library model representing the system under test. In Figure 6.3, we show only two classes from the Library conceptual model. We use specialization to extend Librarian and Borrower such that parts of those types can serve in the test configuration. The test configuration is shown as a UML composite structure diagram depicting the internal structure of the test context, called LibraryTestContext in this case. Since we may also want to acquire books from remote libraries, we show two Library objects–one home library and one remote library. They are both objects of the same type.

Step 3. From the behavioral descriptions shown in Figures 3.7, 3.8, 3.9, and 3.10, we can now derive functional test cases in a fairly easy manner. In doing so, we have the choice of either (i) modifying the interaction diagrams by identifying the objects of the test architecture and adding data and exception handling information, as well as the verdict assessment, or (ii) merely refer to the given utilities in the new definitions of the test cases.

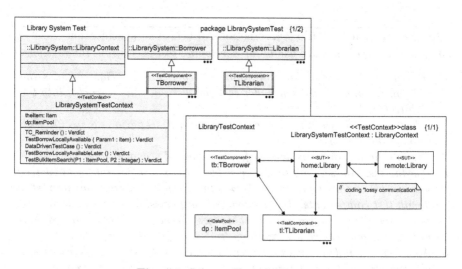

Fig. 6.3. Library Test architecture

Step 4. For the system level test of our library example, both choices will result in test case descriptions like the one shown in Figure 6.4. This test case checks the part of the borrowing an item use case, where the item is available in the home library. We have not yet formally defined the data partitions, so we only informally state that our value of *theItem* is such that it is available locally at the home library. Following the *TestBorrowLocallyAvailable* interaction, such a situation should lead to the continuation *ItemBorrowed* where both the borrower and the librarian will issue a pass verdict. Thus, the test case verdict will be pass.

Figure 6.4 also illustrates the use of timers, with all actions related to timers occurring on the TBorrower instance. Reading from the top, the first action appears as an hourglass and starts timer T1. At the time T1 is started, an expiration time will be given to the timer. Should the timer not be stopped prior to the expiration time, a timeout action will occur. This is handled in the default in Figure 6.5 and will result in a verdict of fail. Timer T2 works in a similar manner.

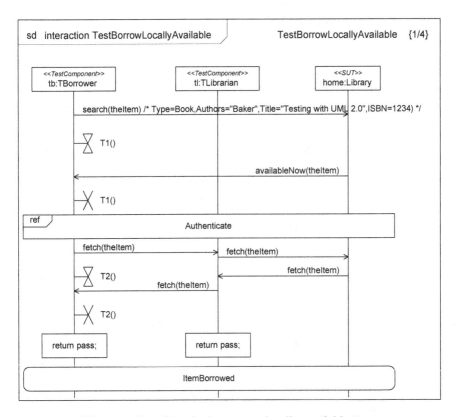

Fig. 6.4. Test Case for borrowing locally available items

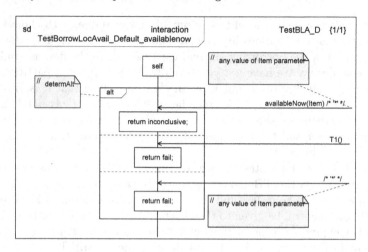

Fig. 6.5. Default behavior on TBorrower instance if the item is not available now

---

⚓ **UTP Concept 8** Timer and timezone

Timers are mechanisms that generate a timeout event when a specified time interval has expired relative to a given instant (usually the instant when the timer is started). Timers belong to test components. A timezone is a grouping mechanism for test components. Each test component belongs to a given timezone. Test components in the same timezone have the same time.

Step 5. Defaults provide a way to respond to messages that are not explicitly modeled in a behavioral diagram. At the messages *availablenow(theItem)* and *Item(theItem)*, event specific defaults are attached to the TBorrower instance. These defaults are called *TestBorrowLocallyAvailable_ Default_ availablenow* and *TestBorrowLocallyAvailable_ Default_ Item*. The behavior of the defaults is shown in Figures 6.5 and 6.6. In these default diagrams, we applied the UTP-specific operator determAlt to describe the alternatives. By this, we are able to define the order in which the alternatives are considered which makes it possible to use generic terms like any message symbol, denoted by an asterisk.

⚓ **UTP Concept 9** Default

Defaults provide a mechanism for specifying how to respond to the receipt of messages that are not explicitly modeled in the specification. They are typically used for exception handling and can be applied at many levels of modeling within the profile.

Figure 6.5 shows the default behavior when message *availablenow(theItem)* is not sent to TBorrower. There, three alternative behaviors are specified. In the first alternative, TBorrower gets the correct message, but with another parameter than *theItem*. In this case, the test result becomes inconclusive. In the second alternative, the timer *T1*, which is started in the test case, times out before the expected event *availablenow(theItem)* comes. In this case, the verdict is set to fail. In the last case, any unexpected message is caught and the test result concludes to fail.

Figure 6.6 shows the default behavior specific to the *Item(theItem)* on TBorrower instance. Again, three alternative behaviors are specified. In the first alternative, the verdict is set to inconclusive when the correct message with wrong parameter is sent to TBorrower. In the second and third alternatives, the verdict is set to fail when the timer *T2* times out and when any kind of unexpected message other than *Item(theItem)* is sent to TBorrower.

A second test case example is shown in Figure 6.7. It is a slightly more elaborated scheme where the assumption is that *theItem* will be available at the home library later. The test case shows the test situation leading to a pass from both TBorrower and TLibrarian.

The default behavior is attached to message *availablelater(theItem)* on the TBorrower instance, illustrated in Figure 6.8. This default catches the *availablelater* message with any kind of parameter other than *theItem* and sets the verdict to inconclusive. In the other cases, such as when the timer T1 times out or an unknown message is sent to TBorrower, the verdict is set to fail.

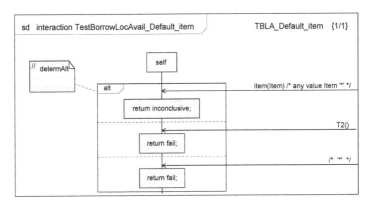

Fig. 6.6. Default behavior on TBorrower instance if the correct item is not fetched

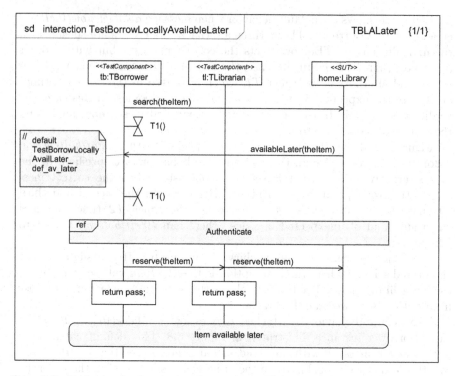

Fig. 6.7. Test case for borrowing items that will be available later at the home library

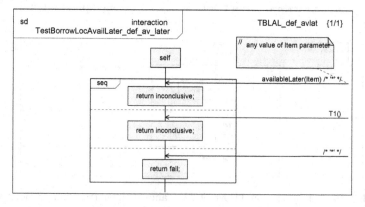

Fig. 6.8. Default behavior on TBorrower instance

6.2 Chapter Summary

Because the goal of system level testing is to ensure that the system functionality meets the requirements of the stakeholders, it is very important to have the test team involved during the creation of the requirements to ensure that they are consistent and testable. To this end, the use of UML modeling provides a means for the development of more precise requirements that can be reused during the development of functional tests. Where different UML diagrams captured different perspectives of the system, careful consideration must be given to those aspects that are important for the determination of functional tests, such as the adequate specification of system interfaces that will be used when testing the system.

Having developed a UML requirements model, we described the derivation of functional tests. We then discussed the importance of coverage, as part of the strategy to ensure adequate testing.

Using the library example, we showed how use case diagrams and interaction diagrams are good for requirements capture and serve as a basis to derive test context, test architectures, test behavior, and test cases. We discussed the use of the UTP as a means of specifying a precise functional test specification, illustrating a range of UML diagrams during its development.

Part III

Advanced Testing Concerns

Overview

Advanced testing concepts, including data-driven testing, real-time testing, and performance testing, are discussed in this section.

First, we consider data-driven testing, where the data values used as input to the system under test are the central concern when designing a test case. Data-driven test approaches are important for GUI testing, application testing, white-box testing, and the like. The test data determined by a systematic analysis of the input and output domains of the element being tested (e.g., the whole system, the user interface). The data used in testing needs to reflect both the important value ranges within the input and the semantic relationships between input and output data. This requires several levels of test data specification, including the precise specification of concrete values, the specification of possible value ranges, and the logical characterization of data. The UTP offers a variety of flexible concepts that support these types of data specification.

In addition to the functional testing discussed in Part II, nonfunctional requirements need to be tested. According to [3], nonfunctional testing addresses those attributes of a component or system that do not relate to functionality, which are reliability, efficiency, usability, maintainability, and portability. In this section, we focus on efficiency, which includes real-time and performance testing. Often, real-time and performance tests are performed once the functional correctness and robustness of the SUT have been determined using functional tests.

Real-time testing is performed to determine whether the system meets soft or hard real-time constraints. Such constraints require that the functionality of the system be provided within a set of time constraints. Real-time tests are typically performed under normal load conditions.

Real-time tests define precisely when an input to the system should be generated and when a response should be expected. The time requirements are typically given as annotations to the system model or in form of separate system requirements, from which the real-time tests are derived.

Performance testing is conducted to determine how the system performs under a particular workload. Often, aspects of system responsiveness, throughput, error rates, and resource utilization are being considered during performance testing. A specific form of performance tests are scalability tests. These tests check the responsiveness of the system under increasing load up to maximal load conditions. Finally, stress tests are used to analyse the system functionality and performance under overload situations. Often, performance, scalability, and stress tests not only analyse the system responsiveness but relate it to the resource consumption of the system and its environment. Typically, memory usage, CPU load, network interface load, and the like are considered during those tests. In result, the system capabilities and its performance under, near, or at operational limits are being determined.

Both real-time and performance tests need to be implemented in executable form so that the timing performed by the test system does not influence or corrupt the time-based behavior of the SUT. This is typically dependent on the execution models used to run the tests, so in this section we concentrate on the derivation and specification of real-time and performance tests and assume that they can be properly executed using efficient test frameworks for real-time or performance testing.

7

Data-Driven Testing

Data accounts for a very large part of system specification and implementation. Hence, data is a key consideration for test modeling and specification. In this section, we introduce three important aspects for data-driven testing, specifically.

- Data types and value specification
- Parameterization of tests and the definition of associated data needed for adequate test coverage
- Encoding and decoding of data.

In doing so, we present how both UML and the UML Testing Profile (UTP) address these key concerns. For example, UML instance specification, together with UTP wildcards, provides a means for specifying values during test specification, leading to more reusable and maintainable tests. Datapools, data partitions, and data selectors provide a means of defining and using data sets. These are crucial for achieving the needed test coverage of input and output parameters for the system under test. Finally, we introduce the notion of coding rules to support the variants of encoding and decoding data during the communication of data between objects.

7.1 UTP and Data-Driven Testing

In this section, we present how the UTP can be used to support data-driven testing.

7.1.1 Value Specification

During test modeling and test specification, testers are concerned about defining data values that are both sent to, and observed from, the system under test. We refer to this as *value specification*. However, during the lifetime of the system, both the structure of data and the values originally defined in the specification can change. This affects the design of test cases, and if data is tightly coupled with behavior specifications, it can lead to a large maintenance burden [28].

Also, during testing, we are not always concerned with checking all the data observed from the system under test. Instead, we are often only concerned with a subset of the data that is pertinent to the test. Hence, a means is needed of ignoring data that is not relevant during testing. To address these concerns, we discuss how *wildcards* can be used to ignore data that is not of concern during test specification and then present a view of how UML *instance specification* can aid the decoupling of value specification from behavior specification.

Wildcards

During testing, we are generally not concerned about checking all aspects of data. Instead, we only concentrate on those data elements that are pertinent for the test. To this end, UTP introduces the notion of *wildcards* as a means of specifying "*don't care*" values. In particular, UTP introduces two types of wildcards.

⚓**UTP Concept 10** Wildcard

A wildcard is a literal specifying one of two possibilities:

1. *Any value out of a set of possible values. This is denoted using "?"*
2. *Either the absence of a value (in the cases of optional attributes) or any value out of a set of possible values. This is denoted using "*".*

In Figure 7.1, we illustrate the class definition for an Item from the Library example. When we develop test specifications, referring to Item Objects, we

Fig. 7.1. Item Class Definition

define *instances* of the Item class. Where, an instance represents a unique entity within our Library system having a specific set of values. However, during test specification, we are not necessarily concerned about the value of all attributes that an Item may have. For example, we may only be concerned in observing books from a particular author. Therefore, we are not concerned about the title, ISBN, or the published date values of a book. To denote this, we define instances for the Item class where both types of wildcards have been used. In particular, *?* has been used to denote that we are not concerned about the ISBN and *** has been used to denote that the Published Date can be absent or if present, is of no consequence to the test. In this case, we would use this instance to denote a Book authored by Baker titled "Testing with UML." Figure 7.2 illustrates an example of the TestBorrowLocallyAvailable test case in which we explicitly define the values for each instance Item, including wildcards.

☞**Tip 6** Use of wild cards within UML expressions

UML does not prescribe an action syntax for expressions. Therefore, when choosing a UML tool for test specification, you should consider action languages that support wildcards within expressions.

Instance specification

When defining instances of Item, we may want to define values for some, if not all, of its attributes. This can be done in one of two ways, either (1) in-lined or (2) using *instance specification.*

1. As illustrated in Figure 7.2, an in-lining approach will explicitly state those values for each instance of Item. When we have complex or structured types within our model, this approach can be error prone, decrease readability, as well as leading toward duplication.
2. To avoid the issues described in (1) we use instance specification. UML instance specification allows you to define the existence of an entity within a modeled system [25]. Using instance specification, we define separate instances that can then be referenced multiple times. In doing so, it provides a powerful mechanism for specifying values for testing in an independent manner. This not only avoids duplication, but also enables the decoupling of value specification from behavior specification, thereby reducing maintenance effort. For example, Figure 7.3 defines an instance for the Item class where both types of wildcards have been used. In particular, *?* has been used to denote that any ISBN is valid and *** has been used to denote that the Published Date attribute is of no consequence. In this case, we would use this instance to denote a Book authored by Baker with

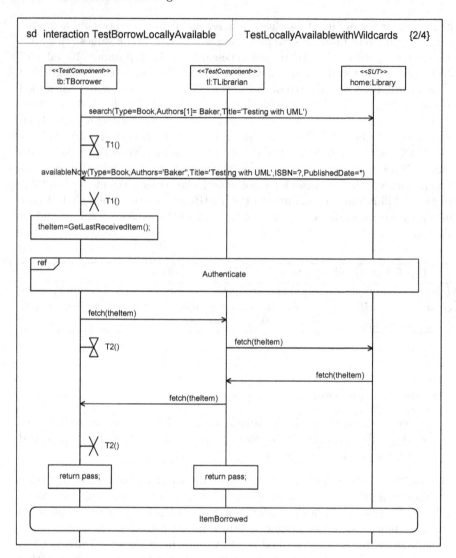

Fig. 7.2. Example of the TestBorrowLocallyAvailable Test Case using wildcards

the title "Testing with UML." Figure 7.4 illustrates the TestBorrowLocallyAvailable test case in which we reference the instance definition for Item. In this case, it becomes more apparent that using instance specification can increase readability and also reduce the chances for introducing errors during the test specification process.

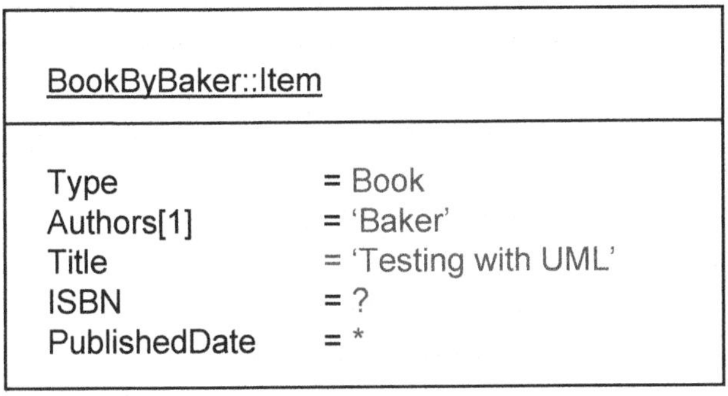

```
┌─────────────────────────────────────────┐
│                                         │
│  BookByBaker::Item                      │
│  ─────────────────                      │
│                                         │
│  Type            = Book                 │
│  Authors[1]      = 'Baker'              │
│  Title           = 'Testing with UML'   │
│  ISBN            = ?                     │
│  PublishedDate   = *                     │
│                                         │
└─────────────────────────────────────────┘
```

Fig. 7.3. Example of Item Class Instance Definition

☞**Tip 7** Decoupling data from behavior specification

Using UML instance specification for the definition of values can both improve efficiency of developing test specifications and also reduce the maintenance of tests.

7.1.2 Parameterization of Tests and Data Pools

During testing, we develop test strategies, plans, and entry/exit criteria that define what testing is needed to demonstrate the correctness of the system under test. In doing so, test coverage criteria are defined that can be formally tracked and measured during the testing. For black-box testing, this criteria is usually defined in terms of the possible input and output values for the system under test. To this end, a number of commonly defined techniques are used, such as *Boundary Value Analysis* (BVA), Equivalence Class Partitioning, or the *Classification Tree Method* (CTE) [31, 38]. Such techniques determine the data values to be used to ensure some sort of coverage of the possible input (and possibly output values) for the system under test. In doing so, tests are repeatedly executed with different values to stimulate the system under test in different ways. To support these types of data-driven testing, UTP implements the concepts of data pools, data partitions, and data selectors.

⚓**UTP Concept 11** Data pools, data partitions, and data selectors

A data pool contains a set of values or partitions that can be associated with a particular test context and its test cases. A data partition is used to define equivalence classes and data sets, and a data selector defines different selection strategies for these data sets.

In Figure 7.5, we illustrate an example of the Library Test Context in which a data pool for Items, called *ItemPool*, has been associated with the test

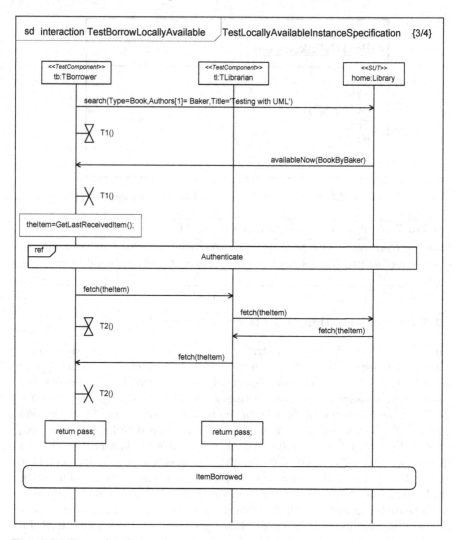

Fig. 7.4. Example of the TestBorrowLocallyAvailable Test Case using instance specification

context. This data pool contains two equivalence partitions for Item values: (1) valid Items that are contained within the Library system and (2) items that are not available from the Library system we are testing—see Figure 7.6. In addition, we defined subpartitions for DVD's, Books, and CDs. Figure 7.7 illustrates some example entries for such a data pool. In this example, we are defining entries for these two partitions such that the type of Items and type of Titles are both different.

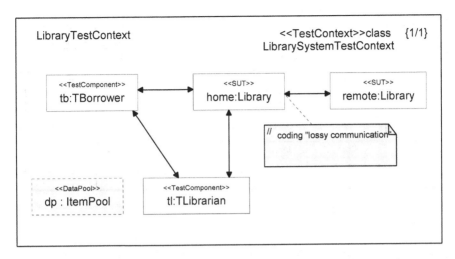

Fig. 7.5. Example of the Library Test Context with a data pool

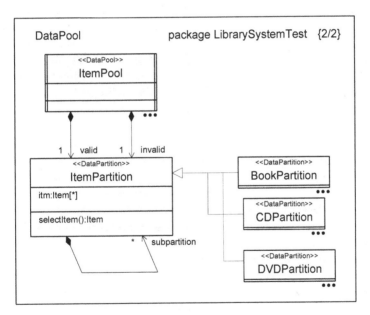

Fig. 7.6. Example data pool definition for valid and invalid Item partitions

Partition Type	Type	Authors	Title	ISBN	Published Date
Valid	Book	"Smith"	"UML is best"	12345	1 Jan 2005
	CD	"Jones"	"Testing is great"	12346	1 Jan 2005
	DVD	"Henry"	"Profiles are cool"	12347	1 Jan 2005
Invalid	DVD	"Smith"	"Modeling is best"	22345	1 Jan 2005
	Book	"Jones"	"Testing is good"	22346	1 Jan 2005
	CD	"Henry"	"Profiling with UML"	22347	1 Jan 2005

Fig. 7.7. Example Item entries for the datapool

In addition to defining the types contained within our data pool, we defined a data selector operation `SelectItem` for each data partition. This operation returns an instance of an Item. Consequently, it is referenced by test cases to select items from either valid or invalid partitions as needed.

To support data-driven testing, we can use values obtained from data pools as input parameters for test cases. Figure 7.8 demonstrates using an interaction overview diagram to provide a data-driven test case that references two instances of the TestBorrowLocallyAvailable test case using values from the data pool: the first reference using a valid value from the valid data partition and the second an invalid value from the invalid data partition.

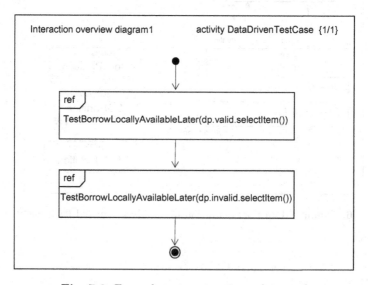

Fig. 7.8. Example test cases using a data pool

7.1.3 Encoding and Decoding of Data

UTP allows coding rules to be defined that specify how values are encoded and decoded when communicating with the SUT. During test specification these coding rules can be used to introduce specific coding schemes that might be useful when testing the system, such as lossy communication channels. For example, Figure 7.5 illustrates a coding rule in which we specify that books transferred between the local and remote libraries can sometimes get lost or stolen.

⏚ **UTP Concept 12** Coding rule

Coding rules are strings that either define how an object is encoded or decoded, or references standards that define encoding rules e.g. ASN.1, CORBA, or XML. They are applied to value specification to indicate how the concrete data values should be encoded/decoded during test execution. They can also be applied to properties and namespaces in order to cover all involved values of the property and/or namespace at once.

7.2 Chapter Summary

Data represents a large part of system and test specification. By considering how data is defined and used during testing you can increase the opportunity of reuse as well as reduce future maintenance costs for subsequent releases of the system being developed. In particular, both UTP and UML provide mechanisms for the important concerns of (i) the decoupling of data from behavior specification using instance specification, (ii) the underspecification of data values through wildcards, and (iii) the parameterization of tests.

Real-Time and Performance Testing

This section considers tests dedicated to nonfunctional system requirements that relate to the timing of the system behavior as well as to the utilization of system resources. Real-time and performance aspects relate to different kinds of nonfunctional system requirements as shown in Figure 8.1.

Hereby [22], *reliability* is understood as the ability of a system or component to perform its required functions under stated conditions for a specified period of time. *Usability* is the ease with which a user can learn to operate, prepare inputs for, and interpret outputs of a system or component. *Efficiency* is the degree to which a system or component performs its designated functions with minimum consumption of resources including CPU, memory, I/O, peripherals, or network resources. *Adaptability* is the degree to which a system or component facilitates the incorporation of changes once the nature of the desired change has been determined. *Portability* refers to the ease with which

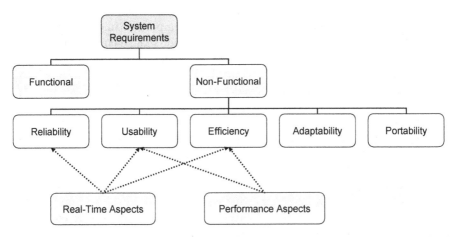

Fig. 8.1. System requirements and their relation to real-time and performance aspects

a system or component can be transferred from one hardware or software environment to another.

The timing of the system behavior influences in particular

- the reliability of a system by, for example, providing timely recovering reactions to erroneous situations,
- its usability by, for example, providing timely responses to user requests, and
- its efficiency by, for example, invoking system resources for a limited time.

Performance aspects relate by definition not only to the system efficiency but also to the system usability as the overall system performance influences the user interaction with the system. By that, real-time and performance-oriented tests are special kinds of nonfunctional tests as shown in Figure 8.2.

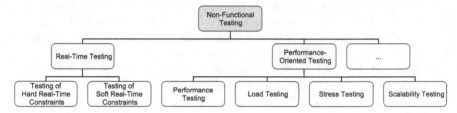

Fig. 8.2. Classification of nonfunctional tests

8.1 Real-Time Testing Concerns

Real-time tests focus on real-time systems such as embedded and/or distributed systems, which are becoming even more important in daily life. Real-time systems are used in business and administration (e.g., e-commerce), home use (e.g., home brokerage), teaching (e.g., tele-teaching and tele -tutoring), and process control (e.g., air traffic control). We separate real-time tests into tests for *hard real-time constraints* and for *soft real-time constraints.*

Hard real-time constraints have to be fulfilled by a system in any case. Systems with hard real-time constraints are often called real-time systems. Please note that hard real-time constraints are not about the speed of a system but only about the fact that the time limits are met. It could be a time limit of an hour or longer as well as a limit in the range of milli- or microseconds. For example, if a hard real-time constraint is defined on the duration of a request response, then a late answer indicates a failure in the system. Other examples of real-time constraint violations that can be more severe could be an aircraft autopilot system, where a violation of hard real-time constraints may lead to an airplane crash. In UML Testing Profile(UTP), hard real-time requirements can be described by time constraints.

Soft real-time constraints need to be satisfied in average or to a certain percentage only. In this case, a late answer is still a valid answer. An example is video transmission where a delayed frame might be either displayed delayed or dropped when not perceivable as long as no consecutive frames are being affected. Although soft real-time systems are easier to implement, the specification of soft real-time requirements is more complex as they often involve statistical expressions.

8.2 UTP and Real-Time Testing

When using the UTP for real-time testing, the test objectives and test cases are to be derived from time-quantified system behaviors. UML differentiates between time constraints for time intervals and duration constraints for duration intervals. Both are called *interval constraints*. Interval constraints can be provided

- within interaction diagrams to constrain event occurrences, message and call durations, and action executions.
- within state machine diagrams to constrain state transitions, triggers, states, and action executions.
- within activity diagrams to constrain event occurrences and action executions.

8.2.1 Hard Real-Time Concerns

In the interaction diagram illustrated in Figure 8.3, two hard real-time constraints are defined for the authentication scenario:

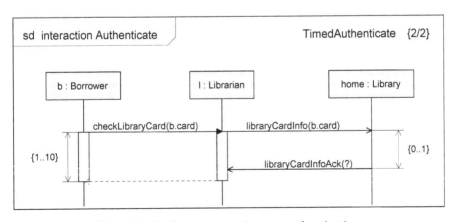

Fig. 8.3. Real-time constraints on authentication

- whenever the *Borrower b* give their *libraryCard* to the *Librarian l*, they should receive a response within *10* seconds—the response should take at least *0.5* seconds.
- In order to provide a correct response to the authentication request, the Librarian *l* passes the *libraryCardInfo* to the *home* library, which takes at most *0.5* seconds to check the data and to provide an acknowledgment.

In Figure 8.4, a test case is illustrated for testing the two constraints given earlier. *TBorrower* is invoking *checkLibraryCard* and starts simultaneously *T1* with *10* seconds. If the call completes before *T1* expires, the test is successful and the timer is stopped, otherwise a *fail* is returned.

☞**Tip 8** Tests for hard real-time constraints

A test for a hard real-time constraint will typically look like the presented one: the lower and upper bound of the time constraint are to be checked explicitly. In the case of time constraints spanning over several lifelines, however, this check needs to be coordinated between the test components being involved.

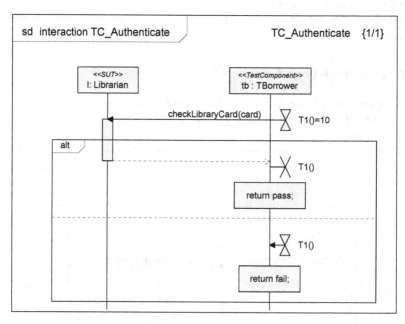

Fig. 8.4. Example test case using real-time constraints

In state machines, timers for triggering transitions can be used as shown in Figure 8.5. in this example, the *LoanPeriod* timer is set to *30* days.[1] In the *borrowed* state, there is a transition to check that the item is not kept too long by the borrower: whenever the timer *LoanPeriod* expires, a transition is triggered. The transition issues a *reminder* message to the borrower to bring the item back to the library within another *3* days. If the timer expires again, this *reminder* is again issued. In real systems, one would use more serious measures if the item is not returned after one or two reminders, but this is not considered within our Library system example.

A test case addressing the correct timing behavior of the state machine illustrated in Figure 8.5 is given in Figure 8.6. Initially, the item *itm* is fetched and the timer of the *TBorrower* test component is set to *31* days. Whenever a *reminder* is received, the test passes, otherwise it fails. One could detail this test to check also that the *reminder* is not issued too early. This works analogously to the test given in Figure 8.4.

In addition, time constraints can be used on states and transitions as in Figure 8.7. Here, the transition to inform about the fact that an item cannot be repaired has to be triggered within *24* hours, while a successful repair may take *72* hours. The completion of the *toBeRepaired* state is indicated by the signal *repair*. The two cases are differentiated by the outcomes for *condition*. Either the item returns to the *ok* condition or it remains *broken*.

A test for these time constraints is given in Figure 8.8. The item for loan is fetched and returned in a *broken* condition. Once it is *repaired*, the *condition* is checked together with the time it took to repair the item. If it took too long in either case, the verdict is set to *fail*.

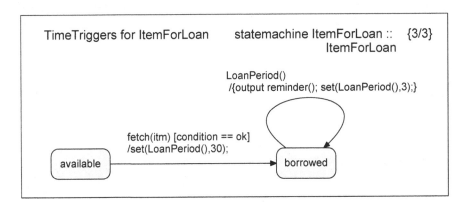

Fig. 8.5. Time triggers in state machines

---

[1] We omit here for the sake of simplicity the handling of time units and the potential transformation of 30 days into 720 hours or into 43,200 minutes etc.

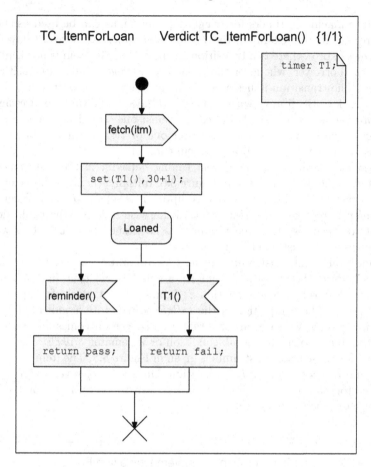

Fig. 8.6. Tests for time triggers

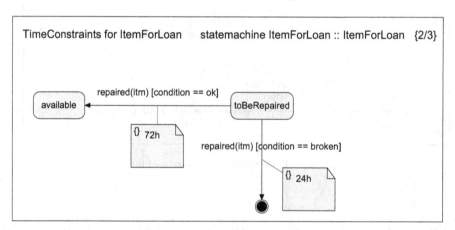

Fig. 8.7. Time constraints in state machines

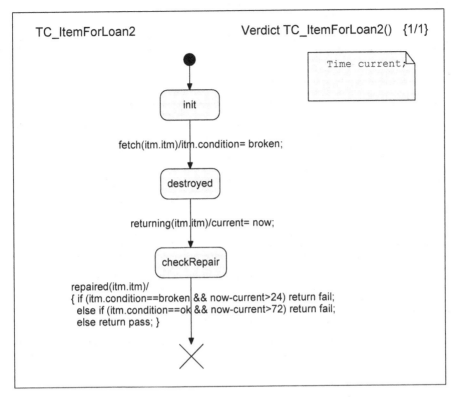

Fig. 8.8. Tests for time constraints in state machines

☞ **Tip 9** Real-time tests with activity diagrams

Time constraints in activity diagrams are similar to timing constraints in interaction and state machine diagrams. Timing can be given for elements within the activity diagram and is tested by means of explicit timers and timing control/calculations within the test case.

8.2.2 Soft Real-Time Concerns

Soft real-time constraints add a probability for the time constraints, that is, the percentage how often the time constraint has to be met. In doing so, constraints attached to elements that have to obey time constraints can be used. In Figure 8.9, the *LoanExpired* reminder has to be issued within *24* hours in *95%* of the cases.

This can be tested by repeating the functionality of the basic test case (as described in Figure 8.2) and calculating the percentage of pass and fail results. While the former is represented by a loop of the basic test, the latter can be done by using an *arbiter*:

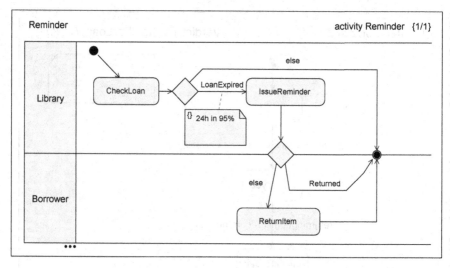

Fig. 8.9. Soft time constraints in an activity diagram

☞**Tip 10** Tests for soft real-time constraints

Tests for soft real-time constraints require the repetition of tests so that a representative number of test results are produced, which allow to check if the percentage is met by a statistically representative number of samples.

⚓**UTP Concept 13** Arbiter

An *arbiter* evaluates individual test results from test components and assigns the overall verdict. The individual test results are given to the arbiter via *validation actions*. An arbiter can be defined for a specific test case or a whole test context.

There is a *default arbiter* based on functional, conformance testing, which generates *pass, fail, inconc,* and *error* as verdict. The default arbiter uses the *only-get-worse* rule, that is, whenever a test component has a negative result, the overall verdict will not be better than this. To facilitate this, the default arbiter orders the verdicts along *pass < inconc < fail < error*.

By providing a user-defined arbiter, this default arbitration scheme of UTP can be redefined.

Figure 8.10 illustrates the repetitive execution of *TC_Reminder* test in a loop of *1000* repetitions. After this loop, the test case returns with the overall verdict provided by the arbiter given in Figure 8.11.

The *arbiter* is given in Figure 8.11. It counts the number of successful individual tests in *num_pass* and of unsuccessful ones in *num_fail*. If the

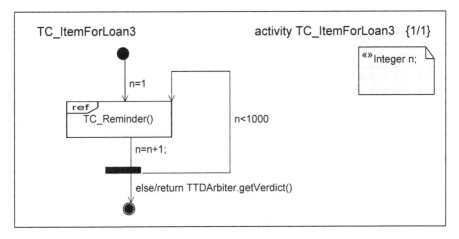

Fig. 8.10. Repetitive test execution

final verdict is requested with *getVerdict*, it returns with *pass* if the *threshold* is met, otherwise it returns with *fail*.

The usage of the *arbiter* by the test case *TC_Reminder* is demonstrated in Figure 8.12. The test begins with *BorrowItem*, then timer *T1* is used to keep the loaned item longer than the loaned period. In that case, a *reminder* from

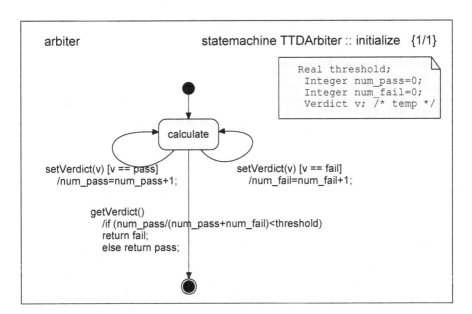

Fig. 8.11. Arbiter for percentage calculation

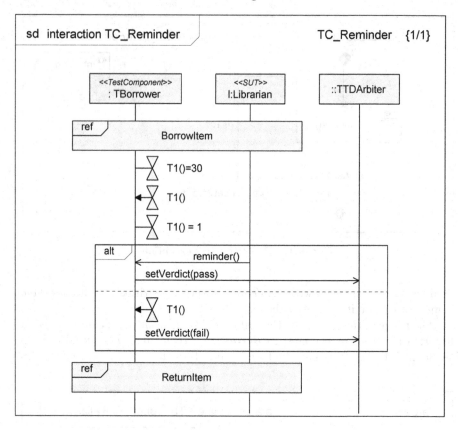

Fig. 8.12. Test contributing verdicts to the arbiter

the *Librarian* is expected. If that occurs, a *pass* verdict is given to the *arbiter*. If not, that is, *T1* expires, a *fail* is given. The test completes with *ReturnItem*.

8.3 Performance Testing Concerns

Different strategies can be used to study performance aspects of a system. One consists in attempting to analyze real load of that system by monitoring its behavior and to derive performance characteristics. The other method consists of creating artificial load and to correlate it directly to the behavior observed during the performance tests. The first method enables one to study the system performance under real load conditions yielding authentic results. The drawback is however that the system cannot be put into specific state and situations so that the analysis of critical and unexpected situations depend on the current load which is outside the control of the tester. The second method allows to execute more precise measurements since the conditions of an experiment are fully known and controllable and correlations with observed performance are less fuzzy than with real load. Both methods are actually useful and complementary. A testing cycle should involve both methods: new behaviors are explored with real load and their understanding is further refined with the help of the second method by attempting to reproduce them artificially and to test them.

Performance-oriented tests cover basic *performance tests*, which are conducted to evaluate the compliance of a system with specified performance requirements. Performance requirements are stated in terms of delays, throughputs, etc., along which the system must accomplish some functionality, potentially combined with a resource utilization threshold that should not be violated.

There are variations to basic performance tests such as *load tests* where the SUT is put under specific load situations. For example, in transaction-oriented systems, load tests comprise submitting transactions to the systems at varying rates, which mimic the simultaneous use of the SUT by concurrent users.

Stress tests are a specific form of load tests, where the SUT is put under high load maximal load, and overload situations. Typical questions of stress tests are if the system keeps its functionality under high and maximum load. It also investigates if the system copes smoothly with overload situations. Stress testing is a determination of how the system behaves when pushed "over the edge," including how well it recovers from being pushed in some manner to discover different types of problems, for example,

- *Bottlenecks:* A bottleneck is the generic term, in hardware or software, for an area in system operation where the flow of data is constrained and causes everything else to slow down.
- *Transactional problems:* Transactional processing is another generic term that encompassed a broad spectrum of things. Generally, transactional processing involves some kind of detailed interchange of information between the site and its user, and often involves something that is processed in several distributed steps on the backend.
- *Hardware limitations:* Sometimes the hardware you have just is not enough to support the work you need to do. Even with all the optimizations and smart coding you can cram into the box, you may simply need bigger iron.

Finally, *scalability tests* are performance tests where the SUT is put under increasing load in order to identify, for example, the maximum load for a system or the point of system degradation if the system is too much loaded.

Performance tests encompass test components that generate load to the SUT. For that, often *background* and *foreground* load is differentiated.

A performance test configuration consists of several distributed foreground and background test components. Often, a *scheduler* is used to coordinate the test components. A Foreground Test Component *(FT)* realizes the functional interaction with the SUT. It influences the SUT directly by sending and receiving messages, invoking operations, initiating transactions, and alike. That form of discrete interaction of the foreground tester with the SUT is conceptually the same interaction of test and system components that is used in functional testing on component, integration, and system level (see Sections 6 and 7). The discrete interaction brings the SUT into specific states, from which the performance measurements are executed. Once the SUT is in a state that is under consideration for performance testing, the foreground tester uses a form of continuous interaction with the SUT. It sends a rather continuous stream of functional interactions to the SUT in order to emulate the foreground load for the SUT. The foreground load is also called foreground traffic.

A background test component *BT* generates continuous streams of data to cause additional load to the SUT by loading the platform on or the network in which the SUT resides. A background tester does not directly communicate with the SUT. It only implicitly influences the SUT as it brings the SUT into various normal, maximum, or overload situations. Background traffic is

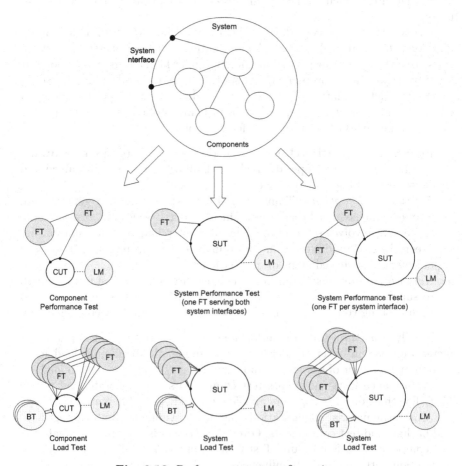

Fig. 8.13. Performance test configurations

typically described by traffic models which are often created by dedicated load generators.

Along performance tests, a load monitor (*LM*), also called a resource monitor, helps to relate the system performance to the system load.

In Figure 8.13, an example system consisting of four components is shown. Two of those four components have interfaces to the system environment. This system can be either performance tested as a whole or individually tested for the component performance. Typically, a performance test for a *Component Under Test* (CUT) or SUT uses foreground testers (FT) only. For load tests, background test components (BT) are used in addition. An LM should be used in all cases to analyze the specific load conditions under which a performance test has been executed.

Along the performance and load tests, measurements are taken in order to derive performance characteristics. A *measurement* is based on the collection of time stamps of events.

8.4 UTP and Performance Testing

A *performance test suite* has to offer features to start and cancel both background and foreground test components to interact with the CUT or SUT. In doing so, the generated load can be controlled and the performance characteristics can be derived by accessing time stamps of events. At the end of each performance test, a test verdict should be assigned. However, the verdict of a performance test should not only evaluate the observed behavior and performance of the tested component or system to be correct or not (i.e., by assigning pass or fail, respectively) but also return the measured performance characteristics that are of importance for the analysis of the test results.

For the library system, we define a performance test to check how many users can simultaneously search for an item. As this is the primary behavior, we place it as a foreground test component and do not use additional background test components Figure 8.14.

In this test case, we use an item pool that is passed into the test case as a parameter. We use a second parameter for the number of searches for an item. In a *loop* with a parallel fragment *par*, these searches are started together with a timer. Whenever a response to this search (*availableNow, availableLater*, or *locallyUnavailable*) is received, the timer is stopped and a *pass* together with the passed time is sent to the arbiter, otherwise a *fail* is sent to the arbiter.

Behind the scene, a scheduler is coordinating the overall execution of this and all other test cases.

A scheduler is typically provided by the UTP tool environment. Still, a user-defined scheduler can be provided to apply other scheduling mechanisms.

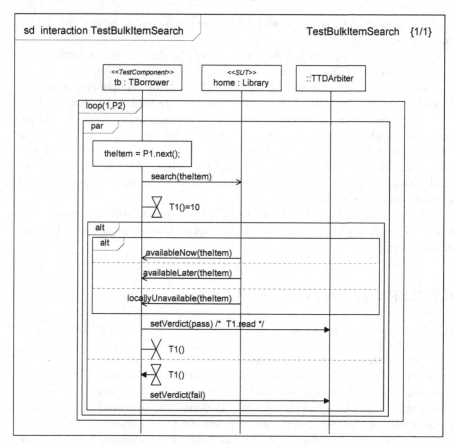

Fig. 8.14. Performance test for bulk item search

⊥UTP Concept 14 Scheduler

A *scheduler* is used to control the execution of the different test components. The scheduler keeps information about which test components exist at any point in time and collaborates with the arbiter to inform it when the final verdict is required. It keeps control over the creation and destruction of test components and knows which test components take part in each test case. The scheduler is a property of test component.

8.5 Summary

Real-time and performance aspects are central nonfunctional requirements for a system. By extending functional tests with timing considerations, they can be transformed into real-time tests. Similarly for performance tests, you use foreground test components with dedicated timing considerations and background test components for additional load on the system and analyze the system reactions under normal, increasing, maximum, and overload situations. A key element of real-time and performance tests is to identify ways of deriving real-time and performance characteristics of interest by identifying those events of the system to be observed and measured in real-time. Beyond this, due to the statistical nature of real-time and performance behavior, such tests should be repeated several times so as to derive test results within some confidence interval.

Part IV

Applications of UTP

Applications of CTP

Overview

In this section, we explore the application of the UTP to two specific application areas: user interface(UI) testing and service-oriented architecture(SOA) testing. The area of UI was selected because of its ubiquity in modern computing systems. The service-oriented architecture area was selected as it is rapidly emerging as the architectural basis on which the next generation of computing platforms will be constructed. Taken together, the lessons illustrated in the next two chapters provide a sound foundation for test specification within these two very important areas.

The importance of (UI) testing is not hard to understand. The UI is the point where the system stakeholders interact with the system, and the quality of this experience is fundamental to the system being perceived favorably. As modern frameworks for UI construction have become prevalent, ensuring the basic behavior of UI "widgets" has become less important than ensuring that the stateful behavior of the UI is correctly implemented, and that the flow across UI elements behaves correctly. In Chapter 9, we provide a careful exploration of these and other issues related to UI testing.

As noted above, (SOA) is an emerging and very promising approach to building the next generation of enterprises and the computing platforms that support them. SOA itself comprises much more than information technology (although the term is often misused as a synonym for web services-based computing approaches). The technology challenges associated with adopting a SOA approach to business are significant, particularly those associated with enabling/connecting the enterprise using web services. Chapter 10 provides a brief introduction to SOA and the technology needs that it raises. It will then focus on web services as key enablers for meeting those needs. Particular attention is paid to the interplay between the UTP and the variety of standards (WSDL, WS-BPEL, etc.) used to build modern web service-based systems.

9

User-Interface Testing

Testing systems that include user interfaces (UIs) can be challenging. This remains true for most types of test objectives whether it be verifying that a UI meets its requirements or checking that a user interface meets key nonfunctional metrics, for example, usability and performance [37, 41]. To this end, we discuss some of the issues that are encountered during user-interface testing and how the UTP can be used to address some of these concerns.

9.1 Issues in User-Interface Testing

Most systems include at least one UI. Yet testing systems with these interfaces remains a challenge for test automation. A UI can encompass many different forms of media, for example physical (i.e., buttons/switches), graphical interfaces, speech, audio, biometrics. This variation introduces a number of issues. For example, the level of abstraction that is used to control and observe a graphical UI will depend on the level of integration between the test system and the application and/or underlying graphics system. If no integration is provided, then test control and observation are based on the rendered inputs and outputs of the system, for example, captured images of the graphical interface. However, if some integration is provided, then test control and observation can be abstracted away from rendered images, thereby improving the resilience of tests and reducing test maintenance. For example, if the requirements for the rendered graphical interface are modified and if no abstract integration is provided for control and observation, then tests will have to be updated accordingly. Therefore, understanding the level of abstraction for specifying both requirements and tests is very important. In addition to abstraction, there are other issues that affect UI testing. For example, we may implement a system that supports different localization options, such as different languages.

Another consideration when testing UIs is the verification of nonfunctional requirements, such as usability and performance. For example, we may want

☞ **Tip 11** User-interface abstraction can reduce test maintenance

Abstracting the way in which user interfaces can be controlled and observed can improve the resilience of test specifications as well as reduce the effort required for test specification maintenance.

to enforce specific usability design principles, such as "when the user presses the 'exit' key they always return to the previous screen," or measure the time the system takes in responding to a user request. Unfortunately, these aspects are often overlooked when system requirements are defined.

9.2 Planning UI Test Activities

In this section, we describe how we can approach test specification in a manner that attempts to address some of the issues presented above. For our example, we do this by defining a conceptual framework for test specification that separates the various concerns relating to UI testing to minimize the impact of changes and maintenance for test specification—see Figure 9.1.

In the following sections, we describe the different aspects illustrated in Figure 9.1.

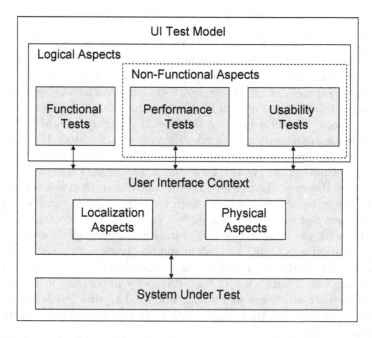

Fig. 9.1. Example of how different concerns can be separated during user-interface test specification

9.2.1 User Interface Context

The UI context defines the abstraction level at which user-interface tests are specified. Ideally, the UI context will hide the following characteristics of a user interface:

- UI aspects that only need to be tested once for a complete product line. For example, testing how a graphics framework renders an image does not need to be retested for each release of an application that uses that framework.
- Physical UI interaction media, for example, voice, audio, graphical interfaces, buttons. In this case, we want to hide aspects that do not influence the core functionality to be tested.
- Localization aspects of a UI. For example, many localization settings for UIs can be treated as key UI parameters.

Hiding such aspects can provide an abstraction for UI tests tending toward resilience and reduced maintenance. In doing so, the UI context is responsible for adapting stimulus and observations from logical tests, using UI contextual information (e.g., physical interaction media and localization aspects), with the system under test (SUT). For example, a stimulus from a test would be translated into a form that can be used to control the SUT. Likewise, observations from the SUT would be interpreted and abstracted using contextual information. The level of abstraction needed to facilitate this type of modeling can be implemented using test agents that interact with the tested application as an integral part of the SUT. It also assumes that lower layers in the translation of control and stimulus can be verified for correctness independently.

9.2.2 Logical Aspects

Here, the intention is to specify tests in a manner that is independent of changes that are likely to occur in the UI environment for a particular product line.

9.2.3 Physical Aspects

In this case, we can define how stimulus and observations are mapped to and from the defined physical interface for the SUT, such as presentation, modality, presentation.

9.2.4 Localization Aspects

In this case, we define how localization variations can be mapped to and from a generic form used by logical test cases. For example, variations such as languages could be mapped to and from "English" as a generic form for test cases.

9.3 UTP and User-Interface Testing

In this section, we present how UTP can be used to define tests for our Library system based on the framework presented in Section 9.1. We choose the *BorrowItem* scenario from the Library model in which a user (*borrower*) wishes to borrow a book from the local library. The user interacts with the local Library web-based system to search for a book, which then informs the user if the book is available or not.

Our library system has a number of UI contextual options that impact testing. The first is that a user can interact with the library system using either text entry or via speech commands, where text and speech cannot be mixed during one session. The second aspect is that the system can be deployed with two different localization options: English and German language support. To this end, we extend our Library model to reflect these possible user interactions. Figure 9.2 illustrates new signals for both spoken and text interactions. Each of these signals can be parameterized with either English or German language prompts/commands.

9.3.1 Test Context and Configuration

In Figure 9.3, we define a test configuration, containing two test components that distinguish between the Borrower and the UI context. In doing so, the UI context test component provides an abstraction for UI tests enabling them to

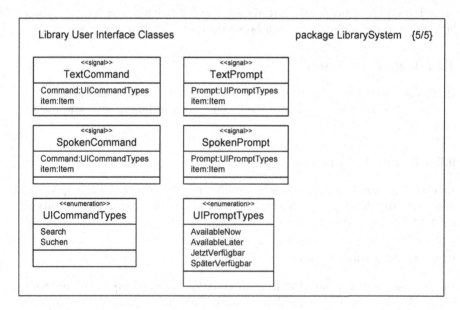

Fig. 9.2. Example of User Inferface Classes for the Library model

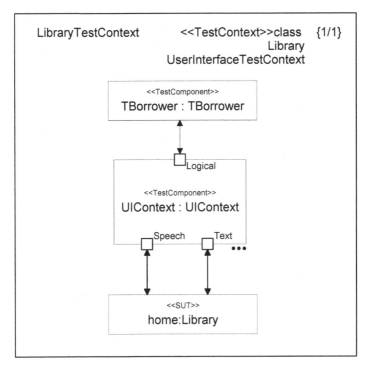

Fig. 9.3. Example of User Inferface Test configuration

become more resilient to changes in UI localization and physical UI options for the SUT. We use different ports to represent the two UI modalities, that is, *text* and *speech*, where all spoken prompts and commands are communicated via the *speech* port and all text prompts and commands are communicated via the *text* port.

In Figure 9.4, we decompose the UITestContext into different parts representing the separate concerns of localization and physical aspects identified for the Library UI. In the following sections, we explain how these parts are defined to handle these concerns.

Localization Aspects Part

This part defines how UI localization options are abstracted away from the test case behavior, by mapping different language options to and from "English" for logical test cases. In our example, we only consider "English" and "German" languages, which are presented to the user either as text prompts or as spoken prompts. The behavior of the LocalisationAspects component is defined as a state machine that takes either.

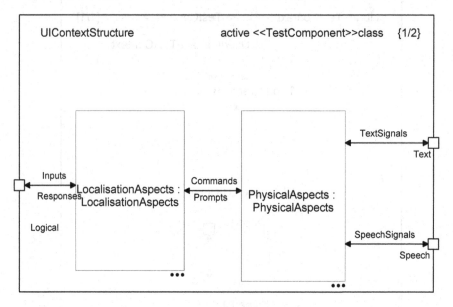

Fig. 9.4. Decomposition of the User Inferface Test Component

1. language-related stimuli from the abstract test case behavior and translates it into the *language* chosen for the particular test instantiation or
2. language-related observations received from the Library UI and translates them into English.

Physical Aspects Test Component

This part defines how physical aspects of the UI are abstracted away from the test case behavior. In our example, we only consider the different "physical concerns." The first aspect is concerned with text-based interaction, where inputs are typed into the Library web interface and outputs are displayed in a web-based textual form. The second is through the use of spoken commands and prompts. In this case, the behavior of the part is defined as a state machine that takes either:

1. stimuli from the abstract test case behavior and routes it to the appropriate port, either *text* or *speech*, which then encodes the test output or
2. spoken or text-based observations received from the Library UI and translates them into an abstract form. It also validates that the inputs were received in the correct form.

9.3.2 Using Interaction Diagrams

By defining a UI context that abstracts away from possible variability in the specification of a user interface, we can reuse test cases. For example, in Figure 9.5, we illustrate how the *TestBorrowLocallyAvailable* test case can be reused from system/acceptance testing—see Section 6. In this case, the only modification to the original is the lifeline representing the SUT, where we replace the SUT with an instance of the UIContext. By doing this, we hide the variability in UI Specification of the SUT and consequently avoids modifications to the test specification as this variability happens.

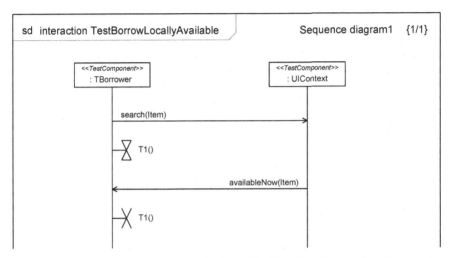

Fig. 9.5. Example of the BorrowLocallyAvailable Test Case for user interface testing

9.4 Usability Testing

So far we have illustrated how UTP can be used to increase the resilience of test cases to variability in UIS. In addition to this, there are other fundamental considerations that should be considered during interface testing, such as usability.

Usability testing can be defined as the process of evaluating the users perception of using a device [21]. In doing so, it may cover a number of concerns:

- **Performance.** This aspect would cover many various types of users' concerns relating to the systems time to perform functions or ability to process user requests. For example, how long does it take to power up a system, how long does the user have to wait for the system to perform some function.

- **Simplicity**. This aspect is concerned with evaluating how simple the system is to use. For example, how many inputs does a user have to execute to perform a function on a website, how different buttons does a user have to press in order to execute a particular function.
- **Presentation**. This aspect would cover concerns relating to the users' perception of the system look and feel. Hence, it can cover many aspects, such as colors, design attributes, and rendering.
- **Perceived quality**. This aspect is related to the user perception of the system robustness and output quality. For example, how good is the system at informing the user when it is unable to perform a function, what is the quality of outputs, such as video and audio, from the system.

In general, understanding what is important for usability relies upon conducting user studies with a sample set of users to understand what key usability attributes are most important from a user's perspective. Once the usability attributes are understood tests can be defined to assess and benchmark them for each system under test. For example, in some cases, standards already exist for assessing the usability of systems, such as SUMI and WAMMI for web-based systems [6, 13]. However, because of the variability in UIs, as discussed in Section 9.1, much usability testing is done manually. Therefore, by abstracting away from these concerns, it will tend towards more effective and increased usability test automation.

9.5 Chapter Summary

As the flexibility and variability of UI increase, it introduces difficult challenges for testing and test automation. Hence, it is important to understand how UI and usability tests can be abstracted away from specific concerns of variability to ensure resilience and cost-effective test automation.

Using UML and UTP, we can define test configurations that provide systematic and logical abstractions that clearly provide a separation of user interface concerns leading to increased reuse of tests. Using the library example, we showed how use test components, composite structures, and state machines can be used to provide abstract UI test configurations.

10

Testing Service-Oriented Architecture Applications

10.1 Service-Oriented Architecture Overview

Service-oriented architectures (SOAs) bring with them the promise of rapid and flexible integration both within and across enterprise boundaries. The ability to compose applications in an ad hoc manner is a step forward for development, but a challenge for testers. This chapter introduces the basic concepts of SOA and discusses the testing concerns associated with SOA. We then introduce a general approach for testing SOA applications and demonstrate it by extending the library example to include services. Finally, we conclude with a review of SOA testing issues and principles.

10.1.1 Service Orientation: Basic Concepts

Service orientation is an approach to providing business processes as a collection of independent services, each of which performs a specific business task within the overall process. SOA is an IT paradigm that supports service orientation. Perhaps the best known implementation for service orientation is *web services*. Web services and SOA are frequently equated with one another, but this is a misuse of terminology. We consider web services as one approach for supporting service orientation. The remainder of this chapter explores SOA testing using web services as a basis, but the reader should keep in mind that SOA can be supported using other technical foundations. Furthermore, a thorough introduction to the issues associated with testing SOAs is an extensive undertaking and is beyond the scope of this book. We will provide a brief introduction to the area and to two of the important issues in testing web service-based systems: determining service fitness for use and testing applications composed from web services.

There are many modular standards supporting the full definition of web services. Three of the most frequently used standards are

- WSDL (Web Services Definition Language)—an XML-based interface definition language for web services
- SOAP (Simple Object Access Protocol)—an XML-based message format that can bind to a variety of underlying transport mechanisms
- BPEL4WS (Business Process Execution Language for Web Services)—a workflow orchestration language for defining flow between services to realize a business process

We focus on the use of WSDL and BPEL4WS in this chapter.

A Brief Tour of WSDL

WSDL is an XML-based language for describing web services and how they may be accessed. There are four primary building blocks in a WSDL definition: portTypes, messages, types, and bindings. Ports are defined by the portType element, which describe the operations that a web service offers. Messages describe the various types of messages that can be sent to and returned from the web service. Types describe the data types used by the web service, and bindings describe the communication protocols used by the web service. Suppose that in our example, the library made the main capabilities (such as searching for, borrowing, and reserving a book) available via a web service. The WSDL for this capability would look something like this.

```
<?xml version="1.0"?>
<definitions name="LibraryServices"
   targetNamespace="http://utp.org/libraryservices.wsdl"
     xmlns:tns="http://utp.org/libraryservices.wsdl"
     xmlns:xsd1="http://utp.org/library.xsd"
     xmlns:soap="http://schemas.xmlsoap.org/wsdl/soap/"
     xmlns:xs="http://www.w3.org/2000/10/XMLSchema"
     xmlns="http://schemas.xmlsoap.org/wsdl/">

<types>
   <schema targetNamespace="http://utp.org/library.xsd"
     xmlns:enc="http://schemas.xmlsoap.org/soap/encoding/"
     xmlns="http://www.w3.org/2000/10/XMLSchema">
   <simpleType name="ItemTypes">
   <restriction base="string">
     <enumeration value="Book" />
     <enumeration value="DVD" />
     <enumeration value="CDROM" />
     <enumeration value="Video" />
   </restriction>
   </simpleType>

   <complexType name="StringArray">
```

```
    <complexContent>
      <restriction base="enc:Array">
        <attribute ref="enc:arrayType"
        wsdl:arrayType="string[]" />
      </restriction>
    </complexContent>
  </complexType>

  <complexType name="Item">
    <element name="Type" type="tns:ItemType">
    <element name="Authors" type="tns:StringArray">
    <element name="Title" type="string">
    <element name="ISBN" type="string">
    <element name="PublishedDate" type="string">
  </complexType>

  <complexType name="searchResult">
    <element name="item" type="tns:Item">
  </complexType>

  <complexType name="availableNow">
    <complexContent>
      <extension base="tns:SearchResult">
    </complexContent>
  </complexType>

  <complexType name="availableLater">
    <complexContent>
      <extension base="tns:SearchResult">
    </complexContent>
  </complexType>

  <complexType name="notLocallyAvailable">
    <complexContent>
      <extension base="tns:SearchResult">
    </complexContent>
  </complexType>

  <complexType name="reserveAck">
    <element name="item" type="tns:Item">
  </complexType>
  </schema>
</types>

<message name="itemRequest">
```

```
      <part name="item" type="tns:Item"/>
</message>

<message name="searchResponse">
   <part name="result" type="tns:SearchResult"/>
</message>

<message name="reserveResponse">
   <part name="ack" type="tns:ReserveAck"/>
</message>


<message name="fetchResponse">
   <part name="item" type="tns:Item"/>
</message>


<portType name="LibraryService">
   <operation name="search">
     <input message="itemRequest"/>
     <output message="searchResponse"/>
   </operation>

   <operation name="reserve">
     <input message="itemRequest"/>
     <output message="reserveResponse"/>
   </operation>

   <operation name="fetch">
     <input message="itemRequest"/>
     <output message="fetchResponse"/>
   </operation>
</portType>


</definitions>
```

A brief explanation is helpful to understand this example. The WSDL begins with the definitions tag, which indicates that definitions of service(s) follow. The attributes in this tag define both the target namespace for this definition, and a set of namespaces used by the definition. Next is the types section, which is where types used in the WSDL are defined. The types show definitions for items, as well as some of the complex content for messages between the service provider and the requester. Next, four messages are defined. The first one defines an item request, which can be used in all three service operations. The next three are responses for searching, reserving, and borrowing an item, respectively. Finally, the service is defined and shown supporting three operations: searching for an item, reserving an item, and borrowing an item. More information on WSDL can be found at http://www.w3.org/TR/wsdl.

Orchestration with BPEL4WS

Given a set of web services, the key to making them useful is the ability to combine them to achieve some goal. This is often referred to as *orchestration*, and is the primary concern of BPEL4WS (Business Process Execution Language for Web Services). We use BPEL as shorthand for BPEL4WS. BPEL relies on services being well defined in WSDL and uses the concepts from WSDL as a basis for defining a business process.

The basic concepts involved in a BPEL definition are processes, partners, variables, and activities. There are many other concepts in the BPEL definition that are beyond the scope of this discussion. The process element is the top level element in a BPEL definition and defines the namespaces that the process definition uses in specifying the process. Partners are elements that describe the various parties involved in the process. Each partner is characterized by a given service link type, which is also an element in WSDL definition for a service, and indirectly associates a partner with a given portType. The partners communicate with the process via the WSDL operations defined for each partner. Variables are elements in which the contents of a message can be stored. They are used for moving information between service definitions in a process. Finally, activities are the elements of action within a process. They come in many types, with the most frequently used types being receiving a message from a partner (receive activity), invoking a message on a partner (invoke activity), and returning a result to a partner (return activity).

Below, we present an example of a BPEL definition that illustrates the process of a customer interacting with his/her local library to search for and borrow a book. If the book is not locally available, the local library searches at a remote library, and if the book is found, borrows it on behalf of the customer. The basis for this BPEL is the WSDL presented earlier for the LibraryServices. Because a full view of BPEL4WS is beyond the scope of this book, the example is partial but sufficient to illustrate our testing concerns.

```
<process name="BorrowBookProcess"
   targetNamespace="http://utp.org/bookborrowing"
   xmlns="http://schemas.xmlsoap.org/ws/
     2002/07/business-process/"
   xmlns:lns="http://utp.org/libraryservices.wsdl">

   <partners>
     <partner name="customer"
     serviceLinkType="lns:borrowItemLinkType"
```

```
      myRole="lender"/>
  <partner name="library"
    serviceLinkType="lns:borrowItemLinkType"
    partnerRole="lender"/>
</partners>

<variables>
  <variable name="itemRequestHolder"
    messageType="lns:itemRequest"/>
  <variable name="searchResponseHolder"
    messageType="lns:searchResponse"/>
  <variable name="reserveResponseHolder"
    messageType="lns:reserveResponse"/>
  <variable name="fetchResponseHolder"
    messageType="lns:fetchResponse"/>
</variables>

<sequence>
  <receive name="searchAndBorrow" partner="customer"
    portType="lns:LibraryService"
    operation="search" variable="itemRequestHolder"
    createInstance="yes">
  </receive>

  <invoke name="invokeSearch" partner="library"
    portType="lns:LibraryService"
    operation="search"
    inputVariable="itemRequestHolder"
    outputVariable="searchResponseHolder">
  </invoke>

  <switch name="check-available">
  <case condition="getVariableData('searchResponseHolder',
    'result') = availableNow">
    <sequence>
      <invoke name="checkOut"
        partner="library"
        portType="lns:LibraryService"
        operation="fetch"
        inputVariable="itemRequestHolder"
        outputVariable="fetchResponseHolder">
      </invoke>
      <reply name="borrowReply" partner="customer"
        portType="lns:LibraryService"
        operation="search" variable="fetchResponseHolder">
```

```
      </reply>
    </sequence>
  </case>
  <otherwise>
     . . .
  </otherwise>
  </switch>
  </sequence>
</process>
```

This examples starts with the top-level process element, which also defines the various namespaces to be used in realizing the process. Next, it defines two partners that participate in the process: the customer and the library. The example then defines four variables for holding the four message types defined in the earlier WSDL. Finally, the process specifies the sequence of activities that are involved in searching for and checking out a book. First, the activity *searchAndBorrow* specifies that the customer initiates a *search* by sending a message to the search operation in the LibraryService port. Next, the search is invoked. The third step checks to see if the item is available. If so, the process invokes the *borrowItem* operation on the LibraryService port and then replies to the customer. The remaining portion of the process is straightforward, but is not shown here.

Mapping UML to Web Service Elements

There have been several proposed mappings of UML elements to both WSDL and BPEL. We use a composite of two easy-to-understand mappings in the following example. This is based on a WSDL mapping found in [43] and a BPEL mapping found in [4]. Other more comprehensive mappings and profiles for SOA area are available [32], but they are more complex and are beyond the scope of this book.

In our mapping to WSDL example, a WSDL port type is defined as a stereotyped UML class, with the operations on the class defining the operations available in the portType. The operation on the UML class also defines the messages. Each operation corresponds to a request message. If the operation has a return parameter, a response message is also created. Types are expressed as stereotyped UML classes. The UML for the WSDL example given above is shown in Figure 10.1.

In our example for mapping UML to BPEL, a process is represented as a stereotyped class, with the attributes defining the variables in the BPEL. An activity diagram is associated with the class to describe the process. For standard elements, the mapping is straightforward, but both UML activity

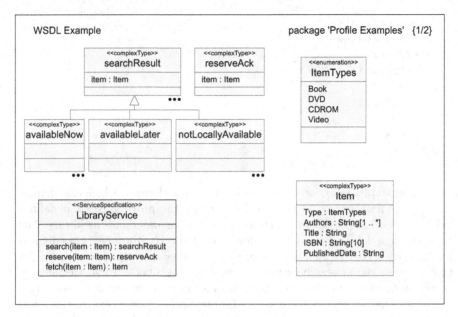

Fig. 10.1. UML model for WSDL example

diagrams and BPEL are complex industrial standards, and the mapping becomes more nuanced as detail is added to either representation. Figure 10.2 shows a UML model illustrating the activity diagram for the BPEL example above.

10.1.2 Testing Concerns for SOA

When building web services-based application, there are many issues associated with testing that need to be considered. The flexible and dynamic character of web services makes the task to testing them well more difficult. Consider the following examples. An application is composed of services provided by several parties, including several third-party vendors. In order to ensure the application will work as expected, each candidate service being considered for use in the application will need to be tested in isolation. Furthermore, the services those vendors provide will each have their own lifecycle for being changed and maintained. Thus, the notion of a fixed release no longer applies, the "owner" of the application needs to be ready to validate that it still works correctly every time a service in the application changes. This points to two major testing areas that we discuss in the remainder of this chapter.

1. Validating that a service is a good candidate for inclusion into a services-based application.
2. Validating the application, including how to test the application "on demand" due to service changes.

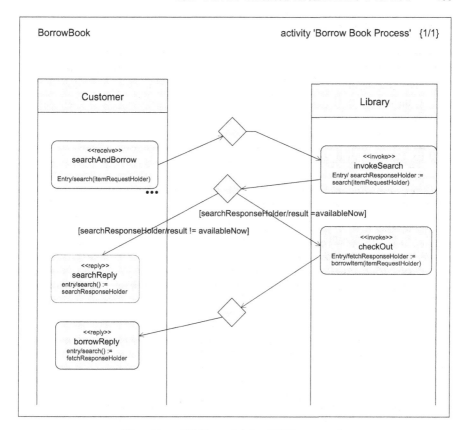

Fig. 10.2. UML model for BPEL example

Individual Service Testing

When considering whether an individual service is suitable for inclusion in a web service-based application, we need to test the service in isolation. This is equivalent to unit testing the service. When performing this test, we need to ensure that we test thoroughly across multiple dimensions.

☞**Tip 12** Testing WSDL dimensions

---

1. *Test all of the portTypes provided in the service.*
2. *Test all of the operations available on each port type.*
3. *Identifying and test the equivalence classes on all of the data elements provided to each operation.*

Business Process Level Testing

Once we have identified and tested a set of services and determined that they are suitable for use in our composed application, we then create the application via process modeling and test it. At this level, our primary testing concern is to thoroughly cover the process. This requires that we address the following concerns.

☞**Tip 13** Testing business processes

---

1. *Determine the paths through the process that we need to test.*
2. *Determine the data variations that need to be tested along each path. These are based on both possible inputs to the activities in the path and ensuring we cover the complex conditions in branches properly.*
3. *Develop a mapping from the test cases to the elements in the process, including the involved services and specific operations. This will be useful for determining which test cases to re-run when a given service is changed.*

We now illustrate these testing approaches by applying them to a services-based version of the library example.

10.2 UTP Test Specification for SOA Applications

In this section, we demonstrate the testing concerns discussed above using the library example. We start by demonstrating how to manage the testing of individual services using the LibraryServices portType as a basis for the demonstration. In this example, we develop a test suite to thoroughly test each operation on the port as well as make use of Data Pools to ensure we cover important combinations of elements in the types provided to the operations.

Next, we consider a high-level services view of the completed library application composed of five major library capabilities. We demonstrate how to test this at the business process level. This includes covering all paths and data variations, as well as providing an example method for tracking dependencies between services and test cases to allow for impact-of-change analysis and rapid retesting when a service is modified.

10.2.1 Testing Individual Web Services

The general approach we have for comprehensive web services testing (as outlined in Book Tip 12) is to create a suite of test cases, one for each variation on a given operation within a port. To do this, we make use of the Data Pool concept available in the utp. We illustrate these basic ideas in an example below. For a more comprehensive discussion on data pools, see Chapter 7.

In our example, there is only one portType defined, the LibraryService port. It provides three operations: search, reserve, and fetch. We know that after a search, we can fetch a book if it is available now, and we can reserve it if it is available later. However, there is a third option to consider, which is that the book is not available at the library (for simplification purposes, we do not consider remote libraries in this example). Thus, to thoroughly test this service, we need to consider these three cases: the book is available now, it is available later, and it is not available. To support this testing, we need to use a data pool, which is shown in Figure 10.3.

Now that we have a data pool setup for use in testing, we can create a high-level test driver that will check all three of the cases we determined are important for thoroughly testing the LibraryService portType. This high-level test driver is shown as an interaction overview diagram in Figure 10.4.

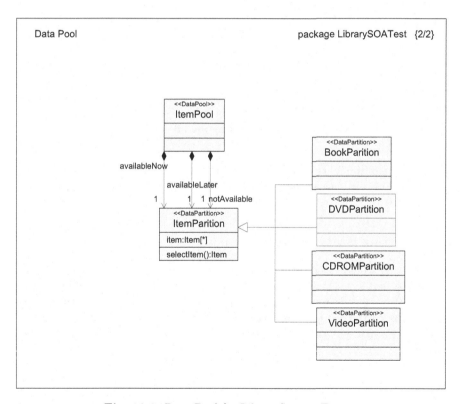

Fig. 10.3. Data Pool for LibraryService Testing

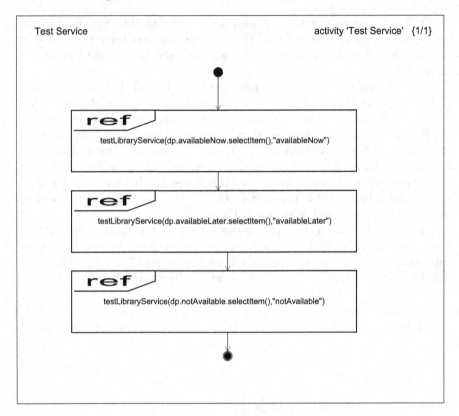

Fig. 10.4. Driver for testing the LibraryService

This driver refers to a test case defined for testing the LibraryService portType. This test case and its subsidiary diagrams are shown in Figures 10.5, 10.6, and 10.7.

10.2.2 Testing Business Processes

When testing a business process, it is the process itself that is under test. Thus, we assume that the services used in the process have been validated in accord with the above requirements. Thus, the service itself is the SUT. Furthermore, any partner to the service which contains receive activities should be treated as a Test Component in order to ensure the necessary controllability of the system.

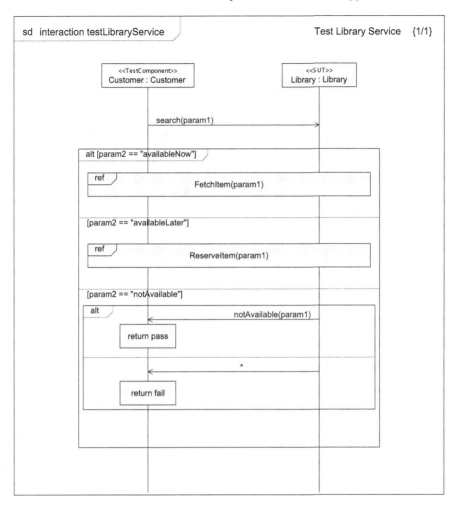

Fig. 10.5. testLibraryService Test Case

In our example, the testing of the process is simple, because there are only two paths through the process, and they rely on a simple condition (whether or not the searched for item is available). Once can imagine much more complex processes and conditions, and the testing required to covers these becomes more complex. We show the two test cases required to thoroughly test our business process in Figures 10.8 and 10.9.

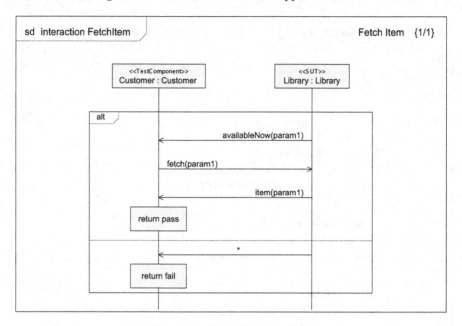

Fig. 10.6. FetchItem diagram

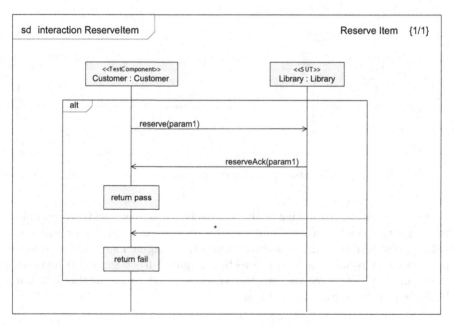

Fig. 10.7. ReserveItem Diagram

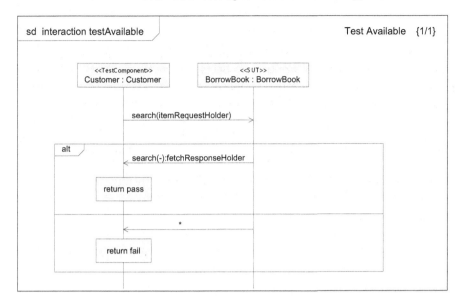

Fig. 10.8. Testing the Business Process - Item Available

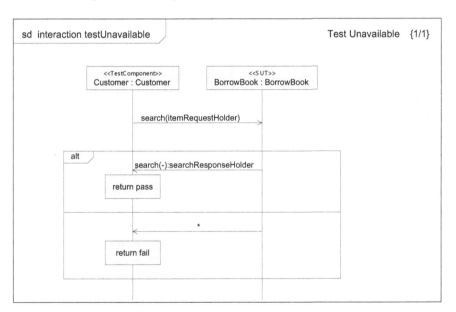

Fig. 10.9. Testing the Business Process - Item Unavailable

10.3 Conclusion

SOAs provide an important new approach to composing applications from independent services. They are rapidly being adopted to support agile composition of applications, enterprise application integration, and the development of applications composed of services that cross enterprise boundaries. They are powerful and flexible, but this power and flexibility brings with it testing challenges. We reviewed a few of these challenges in this chapter and illustrated how UTP could be used to specify test cases that addressed some basic SOA testing concerns. While a complete treatment of SOA is beyond the scope of this chapter, we have illustrated how the testing profile is useful for specifying test cases for SOA-based systems.

Part V

Tools

11

Tool Frameworks and Examples

The UML Testing Profile (UTP) is only as good as the tools that support it. Hence, this chapter introduces the different types of tools and the different ways UTP is likely to be supported. We then discuss two pertinent aspects with respect to the tool support for UTP. The first relates to the interchange of tests in a standard format, by means of meta-modeling, thereby enabling tool interoperability. The second relates to the direct execution of the UTP and the third to the transformation of UTP into another form (e.g., TTCN-3 or JUnit) for test execution.

11.1 Kinds of UTP Tools

Testing tools can improve the efficiency of testing activities by automating repetitive tasks. Testing tools can also improve the reliability of testing, for example, automating large numbers of test case executions, repetitive tests, or distributed tests. There are a number of tools that support different aspects of UTP-based testing. We classify the tools according to the testing activities that they support.

UTP tools support typically the activities described below. Some tools clearly support one activity; others may support more than one.

- **Test design.** According to [23], along the test design the test conditions (in terms of coverage items/criteria) for a test item, the detailed test approach, and the associated high-level test cases are being identified. Test design techniques are used to derive and/or select test cases as outlined in Part II for the design of functional tests and in Part III for advanced tests. The result is a test design document which outlines beyond other things the test suite structure (e.g., by using UTP test contexts and test case hierarchies) and the relation to the SUT (e.g., by use of test objectives) Figure 11.1.

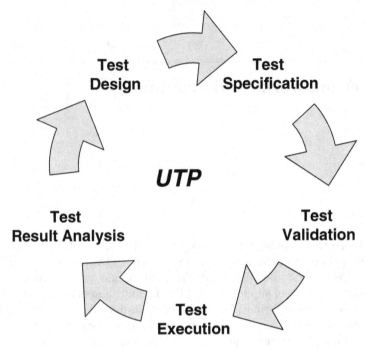

Fig. 11.1. Overview on UTP tools

- **Test specification.** The test specification adds to the test design concrete data for the test cases (e.g., by use of UTP data pools) and test procedure specifications (e.g., by use of behavioral diagrams for test cases). This details the test conditions in the test design specification and how to run each test by including, for example, setup and tear-down procedures and the test steps that need to be followed.
- **Test validation.** Test validation is an activity to check the correctness of the tests. This includes checks for the internal correctness as well as for the correctness with respect to the system specification and/or system model. The internal correctness is determined, for example, by the fact that all test cases are defined as well as the needed test data, that the test procedures do not deadlock, or that syntax and semantics of the specified tests are correct with respect to the rules of UTP.
- **Test execution.** Test execution encompasses all steps needed to perform the tests manually or in an automated manner. A manual test execution can be supported by tool guidance through the test procedures; an automated test execution requires the generation of test scripts (e.g., along the mappings onto test infrastructures defined by UTP) together with test drivers to the SUT. In addition, a test platform is used to run the tests and log the traces automatically. Manual or automated traces are analyzed subsequently. Certain test environments support a test result

analysis during test execution; we however separate this activity to highlight its importance.

- **Test result analysis.** This activity encompasses the comparison of expected versus received responses from the SUT along the tests. The responses include outputs to screens, changes to data and internal states, produced reports, and communication to its environment. Typically the comparison is done by a test oracle, which is defined in UTP by the arbiter and the validation actions. The outcome of this analysis is the collection of test verdicts per executed tests, that is, the UTP pass, fail, or inconclusive.
- **Test generation.** Test generation encompasses all activities where parts of or the whole test specification is generated from a system model along the test strategies determined in the test design activity. Test generation will produce UTP artifacts such as test contexts, test configurations.
- **System model validation.** Finally, tests can be used to validate not only the running SUT but also the system model itself. That requires a test model execution against a system model execution. It is a good means to detect inconsistencies between test and system model in early stages of development and to correct inconsistencies on either side.

There are also tools beyond the pure UTP-based testing activities surrounding the overall test process such as the following:

- **Test management tools.** Test management tools support the overall management of tests and the testing activities carried out. They typically provide interfaces to test specification tools, test execution tools, defect tracking tools as well as to requirement management tools and configuration management tools. Often, they provide quantitative measures related to the tests process (e.g., tests run and tests passed) and the system under test (e.g., incidents raised) in order to control and improve the test process.
- **Monitoring tools.** Monitoring tools support runtime checks during system operation used for, for example, checks if system delivers the required functionality and performance and if it obeys security rules. Monitoring tools run permanently in the background and give out warnings when system constraints or invariants are violated, for example, if a system feature is not available.
- **Defect tracking tools.** Defect tracking tools (also known as bug tracking tools, incident management tools and alike) support workflow-oriented facilities to track and control the allocation, correction, and retesting of defects. Defects may be identified not only by tests but also by developer or customer bug reports. Some tools offer traceability features that link between system requirements, SUT (model) parts, test results, and bug reports to enable a better chasing of the defect correction process.
- **Static analysis tools.** Static analysis tools such as compilers and rule checkers analyze the SUT without executing it but by analyzing its artifacts statically. They can detect possible faults such as unreachable code,

undeclared variables, parameter type mismatches, uncalled functions and procedures, and possible array boundary violations. Static analysis tools can be used for all SUT artifacts, most often they are however used for system code, system documentation, and system models.

- **Metrics tools.** Metrics tools enable the quantified analysis of the testing process in terms of numbers of executed tests, detected errors, severity of errors, and so forth—as well as the evolution of these numbers over time. They also provide means to quantify the coverage and other quality measures of the tests.

11.2 Tool Interoperability

Within a single organization, it is not uncommon to find different tools employed to cover the different activities during testing—see Section 11.1. For example, a test management tool is often used together with test specification tools, test execution tools, and logging tools. Where test management tool is concerned with configuration management and scheduling of tests, editing and analysis tools enable the development and verification of tests, test execution, and logging tools allow the capture and analysis of behaviors recorded during testing.

This situation by itself is not problematic. However, generally different tools exist to support these different activities. That means that tools must interoperate with other tools through the exchange of information. This leads to interoperability problems between different tools whether they perform similar or different testing activities. To address this concern, architectural control points are needed, which allow the separation of concerns, yet provide a means for the seamless interchange of tools without the need for modification. These architectural control points are usually defined in terms of interfaces. Interfaces are generally defined in terms of the information that is exchanged over them. We define this information using *meta modeling*. An example of a key architectural control point could be the exchange of test cases between a test management tool and a test execution tool. In this case, we want to abstract away from any concrete implementation language used for test case, for example, C, Java, TTCN-3. Instead, we desire to have a single generalized form (i.e. an abstract type or model) for a test case that can be subsequently realized in a more concrete language if needed.

☞**Tip 14** Use of standards

Use of standards, open source meta models, or APIs are often an effective means for defining architectural control points.

Meta modeling is concerned with the abstract representation of the information. In this particular case, we are concerned with the abstract

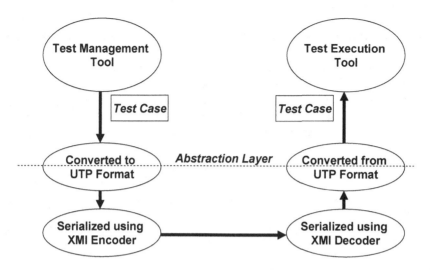

Fig. 11.2. High-level overview of how model interchange works

representation of test cases using UTP as a means for information exchange between different tools. UTP has two defined meta models [26]:

1. one is defined as a UML 2 profile
2. one using the Meta Object Facility (MOF).

The reason for the two representations of the UTP model relates to the different tools that exist for serializing these meta models using XML schemas. For example, a UML 2 profile is encoded as an XML (XML Model Interchange) schema [27]. XMI is the standard encoding for UML models as such any valid UML profile is also encoded in the same manner. Figure 11.2 illustrates an example of the process by which test case information is exchanged between a test management and test execution tool using the XMI serialization of the UTP meta model.

Note that key open source environments, such as the Eclipse Integrated Development Environment [9], use an MOF-based form of meta modeling called the Eclipse Modelling Framework (EMF) [5]. In doing so, the UTP MOF-based meta model is used as the basis for some information exchange between tools within the Eclipse Test and Performance Test Platform Project.

11.3 Executable UTP

In order to make UML 2 models "executable," the models need to be translated into executable code, such as Java or C++. This process is called code generation. Code generation from UML 2 models must be supported by tools mapping model concepts to target language constructs. UTP as a domain-specific extension of UML 2 provides valuable means for functional and real-time test modeling. However, in order to make test models executable, they must be mapped to executable test languages as well.

Driven by the idea to make UTP models executable, existing test languages and tools are examined by the UTP consortium. However, UTP has its roots in different test languages, among those are JUnit for unit testing and TTCN-3 for integration and system testing. For those languages, sophisticated tools already exist.

Figure 11.3 illustrates the application areas of the mentioned languages: While UTP can be utilized for test requirement, test design and test specifications, JUnit and TTCN-3 are mainly used to specify, implement, execute, and evaluate tests during the test development process. However, TTCN-3 can also be used for test design. Thus, Figure 11.3 shows overlapping areas between TTCN-3 and UTP for test design and test specification phases. The application areas between JUnit and UTP overlap in the test specification phase [7].

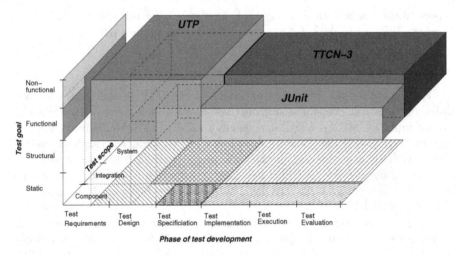

Fig. 11.3. Application areas of the languages

Indeed, mapping UTP models to the mentioned test languages enables the reuse of existing test infrastructures. As a result, a recommendation to map UTP concepts to JUnit and TTCN-3 language constructs is supplied in the UTP standard [26].[1]

---

[1] The standards only give a recommendation since mapping between two languages can be manifold.

12

Test Execution with JUnit

Agile practices have led to a new appreciation of the importance of unit testing. "Test first" and iterative coding/testing approaches have become quite popular because of their ability to help keep code running and of providing a benchmark on how close to working a unit of implementation is. JUnit [16] is a popular, easy to use, and powerful framework for developing unit test cases for Java programs. JUnit played a major role in making agile techniques popular, primarily due to two reasons. First, it made unit testing into a program development task, which is something that programmers naturally understand. Second, it made it easy to create, maintain, execute, and understand unit tests and their results. Unit level tests that can be easily and automatically executed can give quick feedback on the code a developer has written and any modifications to it. This rapid feedback is invaluable for modern development processes. The execution framework for JUnit is Java and the implementations are included in many IDEs, such as Eclipse [9] or JBuilder [15].

This chapter begins by providing an overview of version 4.0 of the JUnit testing framework. This includes a description of how test cases and test suites are defined, how test case setup and tear-down are facilitated, and how to check verdicts. We also discuss new facilities for dealing with exceptions and managing tests with timing constraints. When the UTP was developed, the most recent version of JUnit was 3.8.x. Many of the facilities that are discussed in the UTP standard have changed, and some capabilities have been added that map well to the UTP. Thus, this chapter presents a more recent view of how JUnit and UTP align than the standard does.

After giving the JUnit overview, we provide a mapping between JUnit 4.0 and UTP and discuss nuances in using the mapping. Finally, based on certain profile elements that are missing from JUnit, we suggest some basic enhancements that could make JUnit even more powerful.

12.1 JUnit 4.0 Fundamentals

JUnit 4.0 is an updated version of the popular JUnit framework. The new release is a significant departure from earlier versions, which relied on naming conventions, subclassing, reflection, and similar Java constructs to enable the recognition and execution of test cases. JUnit 4.0 takes advantage of key Java 5 features (particularly annotation) to identify test cases and their related constructs. Understanding and using the concepts require an understanding of the annotation capabilities available in Java 5.0 (JUnit 4.0 requires a Java 5.0 JDK to run). Java 5.0 has a general purpose annotation facility that allows programmers to define annotation types, use annotations in declarations. It also provides APIs for reading annotations, a class-based representation for annotations, and an annotation processing facility. For further information on annotations, please see [14].

In order to understand JUnit 4.0, we need to understand a set of basic concepts. These include test methods, setup and tear-down methods, assertion methods for checking results, techniques for handling expected exceptions, and techniques for timing a test. We now give a brief overview of the differences between earlier versions of JUnit and JUnit 4.0, followed by details on the key constructs in JUnit 4.0.

12.1.1 Annotations: A New Foundation for JUnit

As mentioned above, older versions of JUnit relied on the use of syntactic conventions and subclassing to identify test-related elements and treat them properly. For example, test methods existed in test case classes. To be recognizable to the JUnit framework, classes had to inherit from TestCase, which was an abstract class in the JUnit framework. The test methods had to start with the string "test," which identified those methods as performing a test. To prepare for the execution of tests, the older versions of the JUnit framework called a method called "setUp" which had to exist in the test case class. Similarly, cleanup was done by the framework calling a method "tearDown" which also needed to exist in the class.

JUnit 4.0 avoids the use of these syntactic and subclassing techniques through the use of annotations. Classes containing test methods no longer need to subclass TestCase, and annotations are used rather than specific naming techniques for identifying test methods, setup and tear-down methods, and other testing constructs. We now describe each of these annotations in more detail.

12.1.2 Test Methods

Test methods are identified by @Test. For example, if we had a test method in a class developed to test the borrowing capabilities of the library, we would annotate it as follows:

```
@Test public void checkBorrowingAbility () {
    . . .
}
```

The @Test annotation is all that is required to mark a method as a test method.

12.1.3 Set up and Tear down

There are also annotations for marking methods that should be run before and after each test case. These are denoted using @Before and @After. So, you could imagine using the following code to set up before the test cases and tear down afterward.

```
@Before setupForTesting() {
    theLibrary = new Library();
}

@After cleanupFromTesting() {
    theLibrary = null;
}
```

There can be as many methods as you like with @Before and @After annotations. However, the order in which they will be run is not specified, so any order specific instructions should be done within a single method to ensure they execute in the proper order.

JUnit 4.0 also offers new constructs to perform one-time setup and teardown. These are indicated via the annotation @BeforeClass and @AfterClass. The @BeforeClass annotation is run once before all of the test methods, and the @AfterClass method is run once after all of the test methods. Only one method per class may have one of the one-time annotations.

12.1.4 Assertions

Assertions are used to test conditions that determine whether a test method passes or fails. These are accessed through the static class Assert that is part of the JUnit framework. There are many different assertion methods available on this class, and describing these in detail is beyond the scope of this book. A full description of the assertion methods can be found in the JUnit javadoc, in [17]. Below is a code fragment illustrating how assertions can be used. First, the Assert class is imported for use in the class where the test methods are located. The code fragment illustrates an assertion stating we expect to find a book on a library search.

```
import static org.junit.Assert.*;
    . . .
    @Test public void checkBorrowingAbility() {
```

```
        . . .
        available = theLibrary.search(item);
        assertTrue(available):
        . . .
    }
```

12.1.5 Test Method Annotations

JUnit 4.0 provides two new capabilities that are accessed using parameters to the @Test annotation. They are exception checking and timing a test case. The exception checking facility is very useful for testing whether expected exceptions are thrown when exceptional conditions are being tested. The syntax for exception checking is @Test (expected=*exceptionName*.class), where *exceptionName* is the name of the expected exception. When the method annotated with this information is executed, if any exception other than the expected exception (or no exception) is thrown, the test will fail.

There is also a new parameterized way to time a test. Again, the parameter is declared in the @Test annotation. The syntax is @Test (timeout=*value*), where *value* is the number of milliseconds within which the test method must complete. If the execution time of the method exceeds the timeout value, the test fails.

12.2 UTP to JUnit Mapping

JUnit served as one basis for the development of UTP. Table 12.1 provides the mapping rules from UTP to JUnit. A lot of the UTP concepts can be mapped to JUnit concepts. But since JUnit is a framework only for unit tests, there are several of concepts in UTP which are not defined in JUnit. Some of these would be useful for unit testing and could be valuable additions to the JUnit framework in future releases.

Table 12.1. UTP to JUnit mapping

UTP	JUnit
System Under Test(SUT)	Not explicitly identified in JUnit. Any class in the classpath can be considered as part of the SUT.
Test context	The test context is implicit in JUnit. The context is defined by any class containing a test method (marked with @Test tag). Note that because scheduling and arbitration are built into the JUnit framework, the requirement that the context contain properties realizing the Arbiter and Scheduler interfaces is not met.

Test control	JUnit provides a default test control with its Runner class. This can be extended to provide custom test control capabilities.
Scheduler	Scheduling is performed by default using the JUnit Runner class. This can be extended to provide custom Scheduling capabilities.
Test component	Not explicitly identified in JUnit, but classes containing test methods can use other classes as necessary. They may participate in (but not return) a verdict.
Test configuration	Test configuration is implicit in JUnit. It consists of the classes associated with a context (specific class containing test methods) used in testing.
Test objective	Not an explicit part of JUnit, but may be realized as comments on test methods.
Test case	A test case is a method marked with a `@Test` tag.
Test invocation	A test invocation is a call to a method marked with a `@Test` tag.
Arbiter	JUnit provides a default Arbiter in its RunListener and Result classes. The default versions provide methods other than setVerdict() and getVerdict() for manaing results. Custom arbitration is possible by extending these classes.
Verdict	Predefined verdicts are pass, fail, and error. JUnit has no inconclusive verdict.
Defaults	JUnit has no explicit default mechanism. A hierarchy of Java exceptions can be used to support the UTP default hierachy.
Validation action	Validation actions can be mapped to calls to various assertion methods in the JUnit frame work.
Stimulus and observation	These are not explicitly represented in JUnit, which relies on method calls and return values.
Logging concepts: test log and log action	JUnit does not have explicit logging support. However, Java provides logging facilities that can be used within JUnit. More information is available at http://java.sun.com/j2se/1.5.0/docs/api/java/util/logging/package-summary.html

(continued)

Table 12.1. continued

UTP	JUnit
Data concepts: data pools, data partitions, and data selectors	There are no special JUnit constructs for these concepts. They can all be supported as regular Java classes.
Data concepts: wild-cards and coding rules	JUnit does not support wildcards or coding rules.
Timer	Managed using timeout parameters on @Test tags. JUnit timing capabilities only have one level of granularity (the method) and cannot be used for more or less granular purposes.
Timezone	JUnit does not support timezone.
Deployment concepts (test node and test artifact)	Deployment is outside of the scope of JUnit.

12.3 UTP to JUnit Example

We now present an example of the derivation of a JUnit test from a UTP specification. Figure 12.1 shows an overview of the classes for the library system. These are the same classes as presented in the introduction to the library example, but they have been modified to replace signals for the various library capabilities with operations rather than signals. This is because Java and JUnit are method (operation) based, rather than signal based.

Following the library description is a unit test specification for checking whether an item known to be held in the library can be borrowed or reserved. This is represented as an interaction diagram that describes the interaction between a library testing context (LibraryUnitTest) and a class under test (Library) Figure 12.2.

We now show the corresponding JUnit code. The correspondence between the specified UTP testcase and the JUnit code is straightforward.

```
package utp.junitExample;

import org.junit.Test;
import static org.junit.Assert.*;
import junit.framework.JUnit4TestAdapter;

public class LibraryUnitTest {

    public enum Result { AVAILABLE, BORROWED, RESERVED, UNAVAILABLE }

    @Test public void itemForLoan() {
        String itemName = "An item held by the library";
        Library theLibrary = new Library();
```

```
Result result = theLibrary.search(itemName);
if (result == AVAILABLE) {
   Boolean theItem = theLibrary.fetch(itemName);
   assertTrue("Item should be borrowed",theItem);
else if (result == BORROWED) {
   result = theLibrary.reserve(itemName);
   assertEquals("Item should be reserved",
     (new Float(result)).doubleValue(),
     (new Float(RESERVED)).doubleValue());
}
   else fail("Item should have been held in the library!");
}
//support running JUnit 4 tests with older runners.
public static junit.framework.Test suite() {
   return new JUnit4TestAdapter(LibraryUnitTestContext.class);
}
}
```

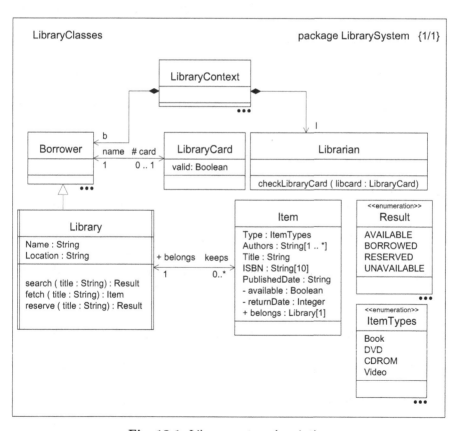

Fig. 12.1. Library system description

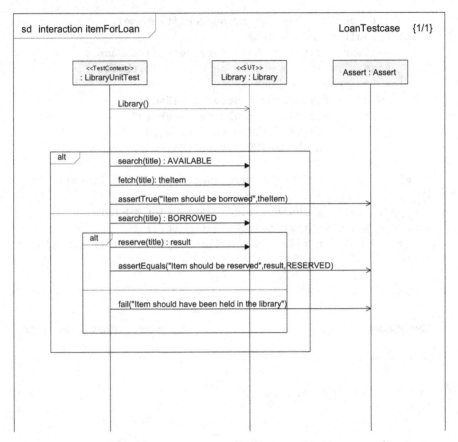

Fig. 12.2. Test case—interaction diagram

12.4 Conclusion

In this chapter, we have provided a brief introduction to the JUnit 4.0 framework and demonstrated how UTP specifications can be mapped into JUnit. To date, no automated tools exist for generating JUnit test cases from UTP specifications, but such a tool could be a powerful asset, as it could unify model-driven development and test first design methodologies.

13

Test Execution with TTCN-3

The *Testing and Test Control Notation* (TTCN-3, [11]) is a widely established standardized test technology for testing communication-based systems. It provides concepts suitable for various kinds of testing of distributed and non-distributed systems. The mapping from UTP to TTCN-3 is used to enable the execution of UTP tests on TTCN-3 test infrastructures. Furthermore, not only can the test execution be automated, but also a precise TTCN-3 semantics is given to UTP test specifications.

Although TTCN-3 was one basis for the development of UTP, they still differ in several respects. The Testing Profile is targeted at UML providing selected extensions to the features of TTCN-3 as well as restricting/omitting other TTCN-3 features. Still, a mapping from the Testing Profile to TTCN-3-and the other way around is possible with certain restrictions.

This chapter discusses the relation between UTP and TTCN-3 and outlines an approach how to make use of TTCN-3-based test environments for the automated execution of UTP tests.

13.1 Fundamentals of TTCN-3

Like UTP, TTCN-3 enables the specification of tests at an abstract level by focusing on the definition of the test cases rather than on the test system adaptation and execution. TTCN-3 enables a systematic and specification-based test development for various kinds of tests, including the functional, scalability, load, interoperability, robustness, regression, system, and integration testing [8]. TTCN-3 was developed from 1998 to 2001 by a team of *European Telecommunications Standards Institute* (ETSI) experts as a successor language to *Tree and Tabular Combined Notation* (TTCN-2). It has been continuously maintained since then.

An overview on TTCN-3 can be found in Figure 13.1: Despite the textual TTCN-3 *Core Language, Textual Presentation Format of TTCN-3* (CL), presentation formats can also be taken as front ends of the language. The tabular and graphical formats called *Tabular Presentation Format of TTCN-3* (TFT)

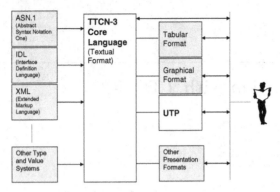

Fig. 13.1. Overview on TTCN-3

and *Graphical Presentation Format of TTCN-3* (GFT) are standardized formats of TTCN-3. Other presentation formats can be added according to the needs of the users. Furthermore,the core language of TTCN-3 provides interfaces to referenced data which are defined in other description languages. For that, types and values such as defined in the *Abstract Syntax Notation One* (ASN.1) or *Interface Definition Language* (IDL) can be imported to TTCN-3.

The ETSI standard for TTCN-3 currently comprises eight parts:

1. The *Core Language, Textual Presentation Format of TTCN-3* (CL) introduces the test-specific constructs of TTCN-3 and defines the textual syntax of TTCN-3 [11, 12].
2. *Tabular Presentation Format of TTCN-3* (TFT) defines a presentation format based on a collection of tables and resembles the appearance of earlier TTCN versions [10].
3. *Graphical Presentation Format of TTCN-3* (GFT) defines a graphical format visualizing the test behavior by means of sequence diagrams. It is based on MSC [44] and was a central source for the UTP development.
4. The *Operational Semantics of TTCN-3* (OS) defines the semantics of TTCN-3 constructs and provides a state-oriented view for the execution of TTCN-3 tests.
5. The *TTCN-3 Runtime Interface* (TRI) is one of the set of TTCN-3 execution interfaces and provides a platform-specific adaptation layer to interact with the system to be tested. It handles communication and timing aspects of the test execution.
6. The *TTCN-3 Control Interface* (TCI) is the other set of TTCN-3 execution interfaces and provides a platform-specific adaptation layer to interact with the test platform itself. It handles test management, test component handling, and encoding/decoding aspects of the test execution.

7. The ASN.1 to TTCN-3 mapping defines rules on how to derive test structures from ASN.1 definitions and how to use ASN.1 specifications seamlessly within TTCN-3 tests.

8. The IDL to TTCN-3 mapping defines rules on how to derive test structures from IDL definitions and how to use IDL specifications seamlessly within TTCN-3 tests.

Further standard parts are currently under development such as an *Extensible Markup Language* (XML) schema to TTCN-3 mapping, a C to TTCN-3 mapping, a documentation mechanism that supports working with tags within TTCN-3 specifications for the generation of test documentation.

13.1.1 Modules and Test Cases

The top-level unit of TTCN 3 test specification is a *module*. A module can import definitions from other modules, but cannot be structured into submodules. Modules can have module parameters to allow test suite parameterization.

A module consists of a definitions part and a control part. The definitions part of a module defines test components and communication ports, data types and test data templates, functions, and *test cases.*

The control part of a module invokes the test cases and controls their execution. Control statements such as if-then-else or do-while can be used to specify the selection and execution order of test cases.

13.1.2 Types and Values

TTCN-3 supports a number of predefined *basic types*. These basic types include those normally associated with a programming language, such as integer, Boolean and string types, as well as some TTCN-3 specific ones such as verdicttype.

Structured types such as record types, set types, and enumerated types can be constructed from these basic types. The special data type anytype is defined as the union of all known data types and the address type within a module.

Special types associated with test configurations such as address, port, and component may be used to define the architecture of the test system. The special type default may be used for the default handling in test behaviors.

A special kind of data structure called a *template* provides parameterization and matching mechanisms for specifying test data to be sent or received over test ports. Test data may be defined both for asynchronous message-based or for synchronous procedure-based communication.

13.1.3 Test Components and Test Behavior

TTCN-3 allows the (dynamic) specification of concurrent test configurations. A configuration consists of a set of interconnected test components with well-defined communication ports and an explicit test system interface (TSI) which defines the borders of the test system.

Dynamic test behavior is expressed as *test cases*. Within every configuration there is one (and only one) Main Test Component (MTC). The behavior defined in the body of a test case is executed on this component. Additional parallel test components may be created and execute test behavior in parallel.

TTCN-3 control statements include powerful behavior description mechanisms such as alternative reception of communication and timer events, interleaving, and default behavior. Test verdict assignment and logging mechanisms are also supported.

13.1.4 UTP and TTCN-3 Relationship

When comparing TTCN-3 with UTP, the commonalities and differences can be summarized as follows:

- both are test specification languages, but UTP inherits from UML the strong support for system and test system specification. This is an area where UTP is richer than TTCN-3. On the contrary, TTCN-3 has a well-defined approach toward test execution where UML and UTP are lacking a well-defined mechanism for execution.
- both are graphical test specification languages, but TTCN-3 has also other presentation formats and in particular a textual one, which is typically more efficient whenever it comes to technically detailed test specifications.
- both are test modeling languages, but the UTP semantics are flexible and adaptable for different application domains (such as the UML semantics). The TTCN-3 semantics is precisely defined.

We can combine the two languages via a bidirectional mapping that supports

- translating UTP to TTCN-3 enables the reuse of TTCN-3 infrastructures for UTP test execution by providing a precise semantics to UTP, and
- translating TTCN-3 to UTP enables to leverage development of TTCN-3 tests on a higher level of abstraction for test design.

Both are explained below.

13.2 UTP to TTCN-3 Mapping

As the design principles of UTP encompass UML integration, reuse, and minimality, the basic mapping from UTP to TTCN-3 involves both

1. the mapping of those UML concepts that are being used in UTP specifications and
2. the mapping of UTP concepts to TTCN-3.

Most of the mapping rules are quite straightforward. Concepts such as SUT, test components, test cases, defaults, test control, verdicts, wildcards, test log, timer, and timezone are provided in both languages. Thus, they can be mapped almost directly. Nevertheless, TTCN-3 and UTP differ in some syntactic as well as semantic aspects. While UTP is based on object-oriented paradigm of UML where behavior is bound to objects, TTCN-3 is based on the concept of functions and the binding of functions to test components [30]. There are other subtle differences such as the handling of interface queues: while TTCN-3 uses a *First In, First Out* (FIFO) queue per test component port, UML (and hence UTP) defines a semantic variation point for queue handling. A UTP test component can have one or more queues, each of which can follow FIFO or other scheduling approaches. Therefore, care has to be taken when defining any mapping from UTP to TTCN-3.

Whenever a UML concept is mapped to TTCN-3, one has to differentiate whether that concept is part of the SUT or the test system. While the test system requires access to all definitions, the SUT needs only access via interfaces or publically available features. For example, UML *classes* being classifiers that can be directly instantiated are used to specify the system structure. Features of a class are defined by its *attributes* and *operations*, which can be *private*, *protected*, or *public*. If that class defines parts of the SUT, access to the publically available features is only required. If the class is however used for a test component, the full TTCN-3 representation is needed.

Another central element in the mapping is the mapping of namespaces. A UML namespace such as a package, an interface, or a class has a qualified name that reflects the hierarchical scope. This hierarchy has no one-to-one correspondence in the structure of TTCN-3 modules. Therefore, a composed module name is built for each namespace. For example, the test context LibraryUnitTestContext (see Figure 4.2) in package LibraryUnitTest and in package UTPExampleTotal is converted to a module named UTPExampleTotal_LibraryUnitTest_LibraryUnitTestContext. The hierarchical scope name can be omitted, if not needed.

Please note that while the principal mapping is provided in Table 13.1, there are further nuances that are beyond the scope of this book. These include items such as the visibility of elements, read/write access, inheritance, and parameterization.

13.3 UTP to TTCN-3 Example

As example, we use the unit level tests for ItemForLoan defined in Section 4.1.

ItemForLoan belonging to the system under test in Figure. 13.2 translates into the record type ItemForLoanClass. As in the class definition, this record contains condition and itm of the appropriate types.

Table 13.1. UTP to TTCN-3 mapping

UTP	TTCN-3
SUT	The test system accesses the SUT via the abstract TSI. The SUT interfaces result in port types used by TSI.
Test context	A TTCN-3 *module* covering all test cases and related definitions of the test context, having a specific TSI component type (to access the SUT) and a specific behavioral function to set up the initial test configuration for this test context. Note that although scheduling and arbitration are built into the TTCN-3 execution semantics, user-defined arbiter and scheduler can be defined explicitly.
Test control	The *control part* of the TTCN-3 module.
Scheduler	Scheduling is performed by default in TTCN-3. Whenever user-defined scheduling is needed, it has to be modeled explicitly, for example, as part of the MTC.
Test component	A TTCN-3 *component type* definition per UTP test component.
Test configuration	The test configuration is established by use of *runs on* clauses or *create* statements together with *connect* and *map* statements which link test component ports with TSI ports or with other test component ports.
Test objective	Not an explicit part of TTCN-3, but may be realized as *comments* or user-defined *attributes* of test cases, modules, functions and alike.
Test case	There is one TTCN-3 *test case* per UTP test case. The behavior of the test case is defined by functions representing the behavior of a given test case. The MTC is used like a "controller" that creates test components and starts its behavior. If needed, the MTC may control/serve also an user-defined arbiter and scheduler.
Test invocation	The execution of a TTCN-3 test case with the *execute* statement.
Arbiter	The UTP default arbiter is a TTCN-3 built-in. User-defined arbiters can be realized by a separate component or by the MTC itself.

Verdict	TTCN-3 offers the same *predefined verdicts* as UTP.
Defaults	Defaults translate into *altstep*s, which are activated and deactivated along the UTP default hierarchy.
Validation action	Validation actions can be mapped to invocations of internal or external (data) *functions* returning verdicts.
Stimulus and observation	These map to *send* and *receive* statements for asynchronous communication and to *call*, *getreply* and *catch* statements and to *getcall*, *reply* and *raise* statements for synchronous communication.
Logging concepts: test log and log action	TTCN-3 has an explicit *log* statement that corresponds to the log action. Test logs are automatically generated by the TCI logging Interface. An explicit link between test specification and test log is however not supported, but may be mimiced with a user-defined attribute for a test case or a whole module.
Data concepts: data pools, data partitions, and data selectors	There are no special TTCN-3 constructs for these concepts. However, the set of *templates* of a given type can be considered as a data pool. Template returning functions can represent data selectors. Data partitions can be represented by attributes for the templates and other means, for example, functions. Furthermore, these concepts can be represented externally to a TTCN-3 module—where external functions provide access to them.
Data concepts: wildcards	TTCN-3 provides the UTP wildcards as builtin *matching mechanism* (and more).
Data concepts: coding rules	TTCN-3 allows to reference coding rules by the *encode* and *encode variant* attributes.
Timer	UTP timer map to TTCN-3 *timer*s, which have seconds as time granularity (and have to be scaled if needed) and which can be started and stopped dynamically.
Timezone	TTCN-3 does not support timezone.

continued

Table 13.1. Continued

UTP	TTCN-3
Deployment concepts (test node and test artifact	Deployment is outside of the scope of TTCN-3.

The SUT items for loan are reached via the address type which points to ItemForLoanClass.

Listing 13.1. TTCN-3 Representation of a UML class

```
type record ItemForLoanClass {                                          1
    ItemCondition condition,
    ItemClass itm
}

type enumerated ItemCondition {ok,broken}                               6

type record ItemClass {
    ItemTypes Type,
    ...
}                                                                      11

type ItemForLoanClass address;
```

Every public feature can be read with a get operation such as conditionGet. Those that can be changed from outside have also a set operation such as conditionSet. Features however that are read-only (such as for itm) will have a get operation only. Private features such as the timer LoanPeriod are not translated as they are not reachable from outside.

Last but not the least, all signals being sent to items for loan or are being generated (as defined by the state machine given in Figure 4.4) are represented by messages SearchSignal which are defined by user-defined types—in our case record types with a field item as defined in the LibrarySystem (see also Section 3).

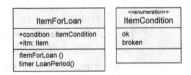

Fig. 13.2. Example of SUT Class

Listing 13.2. TTCN-3 communication to Items for loan

```
signature conditionGet(ItemForLoanClass itm)
    return ItemCondition;                                        2
signature conditionSet
    (ItemForLoanClass itm, ItemCondition cond);
signature itmSet(ItemForLoanClass itm) return Item;

type record itemSignal { ItemClass item }                       7
type record searchSignal { ItemClass item }
...
type record locallyUnavailableSignal { ItemClass item }
type record remotelyUnavailableSignal { ItemClass item }
```

☞**Tip 15** Mapping of UML classes of the system under test

Every UML class of the system under test is represented by a TTCN-3 record. The class features become record fields. For every attribute, there are GET and SET signatures for the read and write access to the attributes. The signals sent to and received from such a system object are represented by messages and their user-defined messages types. The address type is linked to the record type. The classifier behavior will typically not be made accessible by a TTCN-3 operation.

UML classes used for the test system are test components constituted by the test context or by parts of the test context. Their mapping requires the representation of all class features. As the unit level test context (see also Figure 4.2) has no additional test components, just a main test component is needed. This is represented by the type LibraryUnitTestContextComp—see Listing 13.3. This type contains book, which is the link to the system under test and which is created prior to the test. In fact, the test case will run on LibraryUnitTestContextComp, which in turn will create an instance of that type as the MTC, which then invokes the external function createItemForLoan to create the SUT. In addition, port ifla gives access to the SUT as defined in Listing 13.4.

Listing 13.3. TTCN-3 representation of a test context

```
type component LibraryUnitTestContextComp {
    var address book:= createItemForLoan(Book,ok);
    port ItemForLoanAccess ifla;
}                                                               4
external function createItemForLoan
    (ItemTypes t, ItemCondition c)
    return address;
```

The port type ItemForLoanAccess is a mixed port meaning that ports of that type can transfer both asynchronous messages like SearchSignal or synchronous operation invocations like conditionGet (see also Listing 13.2). The direction of the communication is defined with the in and out keywords—for example, the fetchSignal is in out direction as it is sent by the test system, while the availableLaterSignal is in the in direction being sent by the item for loan.

Listing 13.4. The interface to the SUT

```
type port ItemForLoanAccess mixed {
   out itemSignal, searchSignal, reserveSignal,
      fetchSignal, tryRemoteSignal,                                          3
      returningSignal, repairedSignal;
   out conditionGet, conditionSet, itmGet;
   in  availableNowSignal, availableLaterSignal,
      locallyUnavailableSignal, remotelyUnavailableSignal,
      buyNewSignal                                                          8
}
```

Finally, the test case behavior is translated into a TTCN-3 test case UnitTest_ItemForLoan_Interaction given in Listing 13.5. As said already, the test case runs on LibraryUnitTestContextComp. Initially, the item should be ok which is checked with the first call and getreply statements. Then, the item is fetched (withsend(fetchSignal...)) and indicated as broken (with call(conditionSet...)). After return (with send(returningSignal...)) and repair (with send(repairedSignal...)), the item is still broken. Hence, the item should respond with an order note. This is checked with receive(buyNewSignal...) and completes the test.

Listing 13.5. The test behavior

```
testcase UnitTest_ItemForLoan_Interaction()                                 1
runs on LibraryUnitTestContextComp {
   // itm should be ok
   ifla.call(conditionGet:{book}) {
      [] ifla.getreply(conditionGet:{book} value ok) {}
   }                                                                        6
   ifla.send(fetchSignal:{book.itm});
   // itm should be broken
   ifla.call(conditionSet:{book,broken}){
      [] ifla.getreply(conditionSet:{book,broken}){}
   }                                                                        11
   ifla.send(returningSignal:{book.itm});
   ifla.send(repairedSignal:{book.itm});
   // itm is still broken
   ifla.receive(buyNewSignal:{book.itm});
}                                                                          16
```

A more robust way of defining this test would be to activate initially a default in order to handle all unexpected and missing responses from the SUT as shown in Listing 13.6. The activated (Default) takes care of any incoming message (with receive), reply (with getreply), call (with getcall), and exception (with catch) that is not handled previously in the receiving statements of the test case. In such cases, a fail verdict is assigned and the test stops. A more robust behavior would be to safeguard the test with timers; however we leave it to the reader to extend the test case properly.

Listing 13.6. Robust test behavior

```
altstep Default() runs on LibraryUnitTestContextComp {
    [] ifla.receive  { setverdict(fail);stop }
    [] ifla.getreply { setverdict(fail);stop }
    [] ifla.getcall  { setverdict(fail);stop }                    4
    [] ifla.catch    { setverdict(fail);stop }
}

testcase UnitTest_ItemForLoan_Interaction()
runs on LibraryUnitTestContextComp {                              9
    activate(Default());
    // itm should be ok
    ifla.call (conditionGet: {book}) {
    ...
}                                                                 14
```

13.4 Executing UTP Specifications via TTCN-3 Test Platforms

TTCN-3 allows users to specify tests independent of the technology that the target system is realized in. In order to run the tests, executable tests are being generated from the TTCN-3 test specifications. These executable tests follow the principles of the TTCN-3 system architecture which has been outlined and refined in Parts 5 and 6 of [11].

Part 5 of [11] defines the TRI. TRI provides interfaces to adapt a TTCN-3 test system to the SUT. It offers functionality to adapt the communication with the SUT (i.e., how to interact with the SUT, how to invoke its interface, etc.), the timing, and the inclusion of external functions.

Part 6 of [11] adds to this the TCI, which offer functionality for test management, component handling (both on local and remote nodes) as well as the type and value handling (i.e., how to encode and decode data exchanged between SUT and test system).

TRI and TCI adapters provide the glue between test system and SUT. Often, TTCN-3 environments offer a number of ready-to-use adapters or means to generate them efficiently. At the end, such adapters are developed once—possibly for a whole family of systems such as for CORBA or Web Service-based systems—and can be reused for different tests. These adaptors complete the path from UTP via their TTCN-3 representation to a TTCN-3-based test execution.

13.5 Representing TTCN-3 Test Suites by UTP

Another interesting relation between TTCN-3 and UTP is if and how UTP could be used as a graphical presentation for TTCN-3 textual specifications. Although TTCN-3 has an own graphical format GFT ([11], Part 3), this is limited to the single behavior of test components only. UTP however allows not only to visualize the interaction of test components with the system under test but allows also to represent test behaviors with activities and state machines, which is beyond the current capabilities of GFT.

While this representation is theoretically possible, as any correct TTCN-3 test suite is executable by itself and therefore representable in UML (and UTP), there are subtle (but tractable) differences between the TTCN-3 and the UTP semantics. We believe that it is only a question of time until tools provide the mapping from TTCN-3 to UTP. This would be a powerful enhancement, as it would enable iterative test processes with test designs in UTP and technical tests on TTCN-3 level.

13.6 Conclusion

UTP and TTCN-3 are both test specification techniques that are useful in various domains, support a variety of development and test processes, and offer support for different kinds of testing on different test levels. While TTCN-3 is already widely supported by tools, UTP is emerging technology. A major difference between the two is the strong support for test design by UTP as compared to a strong support for automated test execution by TTCN-3. Because of these differences, TTCN-3 is the choice for technical testing and automated execution, while UTP is the choice for high-level test design and modeling. Fundamentally, both UTP and TTCN-3 provide a basis for systematic testing and they can be integrated and used together, particularly in UML-based development environments.

Part VI

Appendixes

A

UTP Reference Guide

Table **A.1.** UTP Reference Guide

UTP	Representation	Definition	Example Reference
System Under Test (SUT)	Element with stereotype <<SUT>>	The SUT is the system which is to be tested	See Figure 4.5 on Page 58, Figure 5.3 on Page 68, Figure 5.2 on Page 67, Figure 6.3 on Page 76
Test Component	Element with stereotype <<Test Component>>	A test component is a class of a test system. It has a set of interfaces via which it may communicate via connections with other test components or with the SUT	See Figure 5.3 on Page 68, Figure 5.2 on Page 67, Figure 6.3 on Page 76
Test Objective	Element with stereotype <<Test Objective>>	A test objective describes the purpose of the test in an informal way	
Test Objective	Element with stereotype <<Test Objective>>	A test objective describes the purpose of the test in an informal way	

(*Continued*)

Table A.1. (*Continued*)

UTP	Representation	Definition	Example Reference
Test Context	Element with stereotype <<Test Context>>	The test context is a stereotyped class that contains the test cases as operations and whose composite structure defines the test configuration	See Figure 4.2 on Page 53, Figure 5.2 on Page 67, Figure 4.5 on Page 58, Figure 6.3 on Page 76
Test Configuration	No special represent.	A test configuration is the collection of test component objects and of connections between the test component objects and the SUT.	See Figure 6.3 on Page 76, Figure 5.2 on Page 67
Test Case	Element with stereotype <<Test Case>>	UTP test case concretizes a test objective. A test case always returns a test verdict	See Figure 4.5 on Page 58, Figure 4.6 on Page 60, Figure 5.3 on Page 68
Test Verdict	No special represent.	Each test case returns a verdict. Predefined verdicts are *pass, fail, inconclusive*, and *error*	Figure 5.3 on Page 68
Default	Comment symbol with keyword **default**	Default provides a mechanism for specifying how to respond to the receipt of messages that are not explicitly modeled in the specification. They are typically used for exception handling	Figure 6.5 on Page 78, Figure 6.7 on Page 80

Arbiter	No special represent.	An arbiter evaluates individual test results from test components and assigns the overall verdict. The individual test results are given to the arbiter via validation actions.	
Scheduler	No special represent.	A scheduler is used to control the execution of the different test components	
Timer	Start timer: ⧗——¦ Stop timer: ✕——¦ timeout: ⧗——▶¦	Timers are mechanisms that generate a timeout event when a specified time interval has expired relative to a given instance. Timers belong to test components	Figure 6.4 on Page 77, Figure 6.5 on Page 78, Figure 8.5 on Page 101
Timezone	No special represent.	A timezone is a grouping mechanism for test components. Each test component belongs to a given timezone. Test components in the same timezone have the same time	

(Continued)

Table A.1. *(Continued)*

UTP	Representation	Definition	Example Reference
Data Pool	Element with stereotype <<Data Pool>>	A data pool contains a set of values or partitions that can be associated with a particular test context and its test cases	Figure 7.5 on Page 93,
Data Partition	Element with stereotype <<Data Partition>>	A data partition is used to define equivalence classes and data sets	Figure 7.5 on Page 93
Data Selector	Element with stereotype <<DataSelector>>	a data selector defines different selection strategies for these data sets.	
Wildcards	"*": Any or null;"?": Any	A wildcard denotes any value	See Figure 7.3 on Page 91
Coding Rule	Comment symbol with keyword *coding*	Data Partition	Figure 6.3 on Page 76

Acronyms

ASN.1 *Abstract Syntax Notation One*
BVA *Boundary Value Analysis*
CUT *Component Under Test*
CL *Core Language, Textual Presentation Format of TTCN-3*
CTE *Classification Tree Method*
ETSI *European Telecommunications Standards Institute*
FIFO *First In, First Out*
FSM *Finite State Machines*
FT *Foreground Test Component*
GFT *Graphical Presentation Format of TTCN-3*
IDL *Interface Definition Language*
ITU *International Telecommunication Union*
MOF *Meta-Object Facility*
MSC *Message Sequence Chart*
MTC *Main Test Component*
OS *Operational Semantics of TTCN-3*
OMG *Object Management Group*
SDL *Specification and Description Language*
SUT *System Under Test*
TCI *TTCN-3 Control Interface*
TFT *Tabular Presentation Format of TTCN-3*
TRI *TTCN-3 Runtime Interface*
TTCN-2 *Tree and Tabular Combined Notation*
TTCN-3 *Testing and Test Control Notation*
UML 2 *Unified Modeling Language, version 2*
UML *Unified Modeling Language*
UI *User Interface*
UTP *UML Testing Profile*
XML *Extensible Markup Language*

References

1. B. Beizer. *Black-Box Testing*. Wiley, 1995.
2. R. Binder. *Testing Object-Oriented Systems: Models, Patterns, and Tools*. Addison-Wesley, 1999.
3. ISTQB (International Software Tester Qualification Board). Standard glossary of terms used in software testing. `http://www.istqb.org/fileadmin/media/glossary-1.1.pdf` (up-to-dateness: November 20, 2006).
4. From UML to BPEL: Model Driven Architecture in a Web Services World. `http://www-128.ibm.com/developerworks/webservices/library/ws-uml2bpel/` (up-to-dateness September 22, 2005).
5. F. Budinsky. *Eclipse Modelling Framework*. Addison-Wesley, September 2003.
6. N. Coleman. Sumi (software usability measurement inventory). Dept. Applied Psychology, University College Cork, Ireland, 1993.
7. Z. R. Dai. *An Approach to Model-Driven Testing—Functional and Real-Time Testing with UML 2.0, UTP and TTCN-3*. PhD thesis, Technical University of Berlin, 2006. ISBN = 3-8167-7237-4.
8. G. Din. TTCN-3. In M. Broy, B. Jonsson, J.-P. Katoen, M. Leucker, and A. Pretschner, editors, *Model-Based Testing of Reactive Systems*, Chapter 15. Dagstuhl, 2004.
9. An open source integrated (tool) development environment. http://www.eclipse.org/.
10. ETSI European Guide (EG) 202 103: Guide for the Use of the Second Edition of TTCN (Revised version). European Telecommunications Standards Institute (ETSI), Sophia-Antipolis (France), 1998.
11. ETSI Multipart Standard 201 873: Methods for Testing and Specification (MTS); The Testing and Test Control Notation version 3;
    - Part 1 (ES 201 873-1): TTCN-3 Core Language
    - Part 2 (ES 201 873-2): TTCN-3 Tabular Presentation Format (TFT)
    - Part 3 (ES 201 873-3): TTCN-3 Graphical Presentation Format (GFT)
    - Part 4 (ES 201 873-4): TTCN-3 Operational Semantics
    - Part 5 (ES 201 873-5): TTCN-3 Runtime Interface (TRI)
    - Part 6 (ES 201 873-6): TTCN-3 Control Interface (TCI)
    - Part 7 (ES 201 873-7): Using ASN.1 with TTCN-3.
    European Telecommunications Standards Institute (ETSI), Sophia-Antipolis (France).

12. G. J. Holzmann. *Design and Validation of Computer Protocols*. Prentice-Hall International, 1991.
13. N. Claridge and J. Kirakowski. Wammi—web site analysis and measurement inventory. http://www.wammi.com.
14. http://java.sun.com/j2se/1.5.0/docs/guide/language/annotations.html.
15. http://www.borland.com/jbuilder/personal/index.html.
16. http://www.junit.org/.
17. http://junit.sourceforge.net/javadoc_40/index.html.
18. T. J. McCabe. A Complexity Measure. *IEEE Transactions on Software Engineering*, December 1976.
19. G. J. Myers. *The Art of Software Testing*. Wiley, 1979.
20. G. J. Myers. *The Art of Software Testing*, Second Edition (revised and updated by T. Badgett and T.M. Thomas with C. Sandler). Wiley, 2004.
21. J. Nielsen. *Usability Engineering*. Morgan Kaufmann, 2004.
22. Institute of Electrical and Electronics Engineers. *IEEE Standard Computer Dictionary: A Compilation of IEEE Standard Computer Glossaries*. IEEE Press, New York (up-to-dateness: November 21, 2006).
23. Institute of Electrical and Electronics Engineers (IEEE). *Standard for Software Test Documentation*. IEEE Press, New York 1998.
24. OMG. *UML Testing Profile—Request For Proposal*. OMG Document (ad/01-07-08), April 2002.
25. Object Management Group (OMG). Uml 2.0 Infrastructure, Final Adopted specification. ptc/04-10-14, April 2004.
26. Object Management Group (OMG). UML 2.0 Testing Profile, Final Adopted Specification. ptc/2004-04-02, April 2004.
27. Object Management Group (OMG). Xml Meta Data Interchange (xmi). Version 2.1, September 2005.
28. F. Weil. P. Baker, and Loh. Motorola Driven Engineering In a Large Industrial Context—a Motorola Case Study. In *MoDELs*, Montego Bay, Jamaica, October 2005.
29. J. Rumbaugh, I. Jacobson, and G. Booch. *The Unified Modeling Language Reference Manual*, Second Edition. Addison-Wesley, 2005.
30. I. Schieferdecker, Z. R. Dai, J. Grabowski, and A. Rennoch. The UML 2.0 Testing Profile and Its Relation to TTCN-3. Testing of Communicating Systems. D. Hogrefe and A. Wiles, editors, *15th IFIP International Conference, TestCom2003*, Sophia Antipolis, France, May 2003, Proceedings. Lecture Notes in Computer Science (LNCS) 2644, Springer, pp. 79–94, May 2003.
31. British Computer Society Special Interest Group in Testing (BSC SIGIST). *Bs 7925-2:Standard for Software Component Testing*. British Computer Society, April 2001.
32. UML 2.0 Profile for Software Services. http://www-128.ibm.com/developerworks/rational/library/05/419_soa/ (up-to-dateness as of April 13, 2005).
33. A. Spillner. The W-Model Strengthening the Bond *Between Development and Test*. In *Proceeding of the STAReastt2002 Conference, Orlando, Florida, USA*, May 2002. : http://www.stickyminds.com/, search for 'Spillner' (up-to-dateness: July 14, 2006).
34. The-Software-Experts. Software Process Models. http://www.the-software-experts.de/e_dta-sw-process.htm (up-to-dateness: July 14, 2006).

35. Uml 2.0 Testing Profile Web Site. http://www.fokus.fraunhofer.de/u2tp/.
36. http://www.omg.org/uml.
37. http://www.usability.gov/.
38. M. Grochtmann J. Wegener. Test Case Design Using Classification Trees and the Classification-Tree Editor cte. In *Proceedings of the 8th International Software Quality Week*, San Francisco, USA, May 1995.
39. Wikipedia. Model-Based Testing. `http://en.wikipedia.org/wiki/Model-based_testing`. (up-to-dateness: July 14, 2006).
40. Wikipedia. Pages in category "Software development process". `http://en.wikipedia.org/wiki/Category:Software_development_process` (up-to-dateness: July 14, 2006).
41. Wikipedia, the Free Encyclopedia. `http://www.wikipedia.org/` (up-to-dateness:July 14, 2006).
42. C. Willcock, T. Deiss, S. Tobies, S. Keil, F. Engler, and S. Schulz. *An Introduction to TTCN-3*. Wiley 2005.
43. D. Pilone with N. Pitman. *UML 2.0 in a Nutshell*. O'Reilly, 2005.
44. UML for Web Services. `http://webservices.xml.com/pub/a/ws/2003/08/05/uml.html` (up-to-dateness August 5, 2003).
45. Recommendation Z.120: Message Sequence Charts (MSC). International Telecommunication Union (ITU-T), Geneve, 1999.

Index